How to Become a

Fulltime
Freelance Writer

How to Become a
Fulltime
Freelance Writer

*A Practical Guide to Setting Up
a Successful Writing Business
at Home*

BY

MICHAEL A. BANKS

The Writer Books

The Writer Books is an imprint of Kalmbach Trade Press, a division of Kalmbach Publishing Co. These books are distributed to the book trade by Watson-Guptill.

For all other inquiries, including individual orders or details on special quantity discounts for groups or conferences, contact:

Kalmbach Publishing Co.
21027 Crossroads Circle
Waukesha, WI 53187
(800) 533-6644

Visit our website at http://writermag.com
Secure online ordering available

For feedback on this or any other title by The Writer Books, contact us at this e-mail address: writerbooks@kalmbach.com

Printed in Canada

03 04 05 06 07 08 09 10 11 12   10 9 8 7 6 5 4 3 2 1

Publisher's Cataloging-in-Publication

　　Banks, Michael A.
　　　　How to become a fulltime freelance writer : a
　　practical guide to setting up a successful writing
　　business at home / by Michael A. Banks. — 1st ed.
　　　　p. cm.
　　　　ISBN 0-87116-197-4

　　　　1. Authorship—Vocational guidance. 2. Home-based
　　businesses.   I. Title.

　　PN153.B36 2003   808'.02

Book design by Mighty Media, Minneapolis

for Bill Brohaugh,
who believed in it first

ACKNOWLEDGMENTS

I wish to express my gratitude to the editorial and production staff at The Writer Books—editor Philip Martin, in particular—for their professionalism and support of this project.

I'd also like to thank my fellow writers who over the many years have contributed to my education in the field of writing—and to my enjoyment of this challenging but immensely rewarding line of work. Being a writer means to be in the company of other writers, sometime in person and sometimes just in spirit, and I am grateful for that fellowship and camaraderie.

And lastly, I've survived as a writer (and simply survived as a person) thanks to some amazing women in my life—my mother, my daughter, other relatives, and good friends. If you know even one of these wonderful people, you are blessed.

Carole Banks
Sue Banks
Susan Banks
Susanne Beeler
Ramona Brown
Patricia K. Cadigan
Anne Curry
Becky Francisco
Marj Krueger
Meredith Mark
Betsy Mitchell
Debbie Morner
Rose Wells

You are each special, and I love you for it.

CONTENTS

INTRODUCTION

WHAT COMES TO MIND when you think about writing for a living? Getting big royalty checks? Having lots more leisure time? Being your own boss? Or perhaps you just wish to validate your work with regular publication?

It's all out there, and you can have it. The rewards and risks, the challenges and learning experiences and growth—all of it.

But where does the route to full-time writing begin? How far must one go and what obstacles might exist? This book answers those questions, and more. It maps the territory: the book and magazine publishing industry. And it offers solid advice on the best path to get from here to there.

This information (with, perhaps, a touch of wisdom) comes to you from those who have been there. To write this book, I drew on the experience of dozens of full-time writers, as well as my own as a freelance writer for the past 20 years. My fellow writers happily joined me in providing useful advice, helping to point out chuckholes, washed-out bridges, and detours to avoid on your metaphorical route to success as a full-time freelance writer. Like me, they have traveled this journey for many years. In the fellowship of the road, we all want to help you succeed—and get there more efficiently than we did. Too often, we learned the hard way which was really the best path to our chosen destination. We want to share that good news—so you have a quicker route, more great scenic opportunities along the way, positive feedback from those who travel with you, and less damage to the vehicle involved in the trip.

All together, this advice provides a practical road map that you can use on your own journey.

What You'll Find in This Book

At first glance the issue of writing for a living may seem an amorphous mass of intertwining topics. This book focuses on three areas of particular interest to those considering becoming full-time freelancers:

1. *Writing and marketing.* The nuts and bolts of writing for publication, including developing the markets for your work. How does this differ from writing on an occasional basis?

2. *Writing as a profession.* What to expect, and how to deal with financial planning, daily discipline, career mapping, and much more. How to deal with setbacks, and how to seek success.

3. *Tales of accomplishment—or abysmal woe.* Whether inspirational or cautionary, these anecdotes come from a variety of writing venues and genres (magazines, technical writing, novels and nonfiction books, and other fields), and they each offer a valuable learning experience.

In support, I've included lots of concrete examples, suggestions, quotes, and other useful aids to learning about writing in general, and freelancing in particular.

What's in It for You?

I can't guarantee that you'll become a bestselling author. Even if you see your work published regularly, you may not make a living in this strange business. Even if you follow all the tips, advice, and information in this guide—as they say, your actual results may vary, because there are a number of variables in how successful one can be as a writer.

The first—and certainly most important—variable is you. You must be willing and able to learn, to work diligently toward your success, and to understand and learn again and again from your successes and failures. You have to motivate yourself. You have to take responsibility for failures and successes. And you must be persistent. I'll give you guidance in all these areas, and more. At the end of the day, through, you are the one who makes it happen for you.

Other variables are often out of your control, from the trends in the overall economy to quirks of how a particular book or magazine publisher is doing financially, or even who is retiring, changing jobs, getting a divorce, or any of hundreds of unforeseen events taking place.

But the key to success lies in you: How well can you blend the discipline of writing full-time, as a professional, with the pure joy of creativity and literary expression that comes from your heart. A successful freelance writer is one who is willing to consider carefully the issues raised—and heed the advice offered—in this book.

And if you are writing part-time? The advice here will help you as well—either to prepare yourself to go full-time in the near future, or just to gain better results in your part-time endeavors.

Why I Wrote This Book

I wrote this book because I've listened to you at writers' conferences. I've read your letters asking for advice. I've been an editor, buying books and stories. And I've shared tales with many other writers about how we got into this crazy business—what worked and what didn't.

I remember what it was like when I first started writing with intent to sell. I recall the self-doubt: wondering whether I was a "good enough" writer. I wasn't sure if I needed to know someone to get into print. I worried that I might misstate myself in a cover letter, or seem pretentious in sending out an ambitious query letter.

Later, with a few books to my credit, I still worried: that those might have been a fluke. I feared that I might run out of ideas. I worried about competition from other writers preventing me from earning a living. And I worried about everything else you've worried about . . .

In short: This is the book I wish I could have read in 1971, when I started on my own road to writing for a living.

Are You Ready to Take This Trip?

As I've emphasized, your success is up to you. You have to want to embark on this journey to become a professional writer. You are the one who will sacrifice, suffer headaches metaphorical and literal, and agonize over ideas and sentences late into the night before a pressing deadline.

But by becoming a full-time freelancer, you will discover how to make time for writing, and how to get around those headaches. You will find the right words and the appropriate sentences. The ideas you have in your head will turn into published works. You will conquer any and all other roadblocks to writing.

I know you can, because I did, and so have thousands of other writers. You already have the desire. Together, we'll make sure you have the commitment and the knowledge you need.

Here's your map. Now it's your turn. Let's hit the road!

—*Michael A. Banks*
Oxford, Ohio

CHAPTER 1

Prerequisites to Writing as a Career

AS YOU KNOW, THERE ARE NO TESTS to certify you as a full-time freelance writer. There is no college degree that guarantees success as a professional writer of fiction or nonfiction. And there's no place you can go to apply for a job as a full-time freelancer. What you are contemplating—writing as a home-based career— is something you will have to tackle yourself.

So how do you get there? More than anything, you get published by writing. Eventually, by writing (and being published) consistently, you get to the point where you can write full-time.

So what's really required to succeed? Certainly writing ability—but we all know folks who are great writers but never consider writing as a career. (In the same way, there are people who are truly gifted musicians, singers, or artists—but never try to make their living at it.)

For part-time or full-time writers, success requires a complex mix of character traits, motivation, knowledge, experience, and more. Let's take a quick look at the major prerequisites for writing success.

Writing Ability

How's your writing? Do you struggle to get the sentences right? Do you feel that your writing isn't up to par with that of other writers you read?

First of all, chances are that your writing is better than you think. We are, after all, our own worst critics. (Even the most supreme ego is self-critical.) And as a writer, when you go over a page or a paragraph many times, you can easily lose perspective. Often you find yourself in a "can't see the forest for the trees" state.

In my own work, I've found this to be true time and again. Certain articles or stories that I thought read poorly turned out to be among my best-received work. One science fiction story I wrote comes to mind; I was never satisfied with it, but eventually gave up and mailed it out. It ended up being reprinted numerous times.

Don't try to judge your work totally from your own perspective. You may be doing far better than you think, but just can't see it. Worse yet, you can end up rewriting a manuscript too many times and losing its best qualities.

If you just can't get a handle on why your manuscript doesn't seem to be working, put it away for two weeks. When you get around to reading it again, you'll find that it reads like someone else wrote it. This will help you determine whether it was indeed your writing style or just an overly critical nature that was at fault.

Of course, everything you write can usually be improved by guiding it through several drafts. Every piece of writing benefits from being revised, often a good number of times. Writers unwilling to do that will remain unpublished.

Ideally, you can tell when your writing is off-base or lacking

The Origins of the Word "Freelance"

The term "free lance" was invented by the novelist Walter Scott to refer to itinerant mercenary soldiers who sold their abilities to the highest bidder. At first such soldiers were known as "free companions." Since they usually traveled with their own weapons (lances), Scott dubbed them "free lancers."

—Bob Perlongo,
in The Write Book:
An Illustrated Treasury of
Tips, Tactics and Tirades

in style, technique, or crucial information. To get honest feedback on your writing's readability, show some of your work to others. And listen to their feedback. Do your words get in the way of what you are saying? To be a successful writer, you must be able to write about many a complex process, thing, or topic. The true test: does your work read well enough for non-writers to visualize what you see in your mind and are trying to depict?

Here is one exercise I've often used in teaching writing classes. First, choose a paragraph from a book or magazine that you enjoyed reading. Then, sit down and rewrite it in your own words—but try to retain the meaning of the original. Now compare the two versions side by side. Have you come up with a new way to describe the content at hand? If you can't write to a level of comprehension and smooth readability that matches favorably with the original passage, you need to work on your writing on fundamental levels.

The ultimate test is submitting your work for publication. Editors always require clarity and quality in the writing they accept. If you never get accepted for publication, you may begin to suspect your writing needs work. Go back to the basics; study the work of the masters.

And if your work is accepted for publication, it likely will receive some editing suggestions. While incorporating as many of those as possible, look also for patterns in what your editors are marking up. Do you consistently over-use pet phrases, for instance?

One of the best ways to improve your writing is to write. Writing is like any profession or trade: the longer you work at it, the better you get.

The other great teaching tool: simply read good writing. Seek out the award-winning stories in your field of interest. Each year there are prizes given and anthologies published. Read these stories as a writer. How would you have told that story? How did the award-winning authors begin their stories? How did they end them? What did they do that was surprising? Focus on the words—their structure and effects—and you will grow as a writer.

There are also excellent books, courses, and magazines geared toward helping you improve your writing. You'll find some publications I recommend for this purpose listed in Appendix A. Just as for physicians and physicists, there are many avenues of lifelong learning and experimentation for writers. Keep in touch with developments in the field of professional writing. The writer you are today is not quite as good as the author you can become by next year—if you are willing to grow, read, and try to find ways to write better.

Knowledge of Subject

Knowledge of one's subject matter can come from experience or research. No matter what the source, it must be real and accurate. For example, I've written extensively about crime on the Internet. My knowledge comes from first-hand experience—I've spent 20 years online. I also continue to expand my knowledge base through research interviews with Internet crime victims, law-enforcement officers, and those who work for Internet providers.

You must know more than you use in your writing. In talking to successful writers, I've found that they always know far more about the topic they are writing about than comes through in their work. This applies equally to fiction and nonfiction.

The saying "a little knowledge goes a long way" is not true for writers. The opposite is more accurate—you can never know too much about your chosen topic.

If you know your subject matter thoroughly, it shows in your writing. You write more convincingly and with greater clarity. The more comfortable you are with your knowledge of content, the more you are free to focus on your writing style, technique, and structure. You don't have to wonder about some point of confusion in your own mind; instead, you can anticipate and answer questions that might occur to your readers.

While you may know a lot about a subject, don't try to get everything you know into a story, article, or book. Doing so will leave you and the reader confused by abundance. Pick a focus, and communicate it clearly. Avoid useless diversions from the topic and theme of the piece. If you know more, just save it for the next piece. Sometimes you can recycle the same information later, just organizing it differently around another theme for a different market or a follow-up piece to the same publisher.

Think long-term. You need to increase your knowledge of subjects upon which you need to write. Do you have a plan to acquire that knowledge and keep it up-to-date? And have you considered which markets want to buy your writings on that topic? How can you use that knowledge to write as much as you can, over time, to recoup your investment in acquiring that information?

Command of the Craft & Tools

Like any skilled tradesperson or professional practitioner, successful writers know their tools. The medical doctor has diagnostic tools, a reference library, professional journals, and tools of treatment. The carpenter has hammer, level, square, and other tools.

You as a writer have tools, too. It begins with your writing equipment, in the form of pads of paper and notebooks, an ample supply of pens, word processor, and printer. Many writers make good use of a simple but decent-quality tape recorder, keeping plenty of blank tapes at hand. Other key resources include stacks of postal and shipping supplies, file folders, a telephone with an answering machine, a shelf or two of reference books.

Most of us today have some sort of readily available Web access, for research and for communicating with editors and interviewees. It's becoming more important every day to have a well-operating computer, free of vexing crashes, with a basic array of programs for e-mail, word processing, and other needs.

You need to know your tools well—including how to keep them in good working order—so that using them doesn't get in the way of your writing.

You also should be knowledgeable about the technical craft of writing. You have more than a nodding acquaintance with the use of the English language and its common forms and structures. What is a scene? What is an expository passage? What's the typical structure of poems, short stories, or articles? Why do books have prefaces and introductions? What goes in the front matter or the end matter?

From the macro to the micro, be familiar with how the English language works. How are words and sentences put together to greatest effect? How did classic essayists such as E. B. White do it? And why did James Joyce or Hunter Thompson become famous by writing in ways that were surprisingly different? Learn to love words, to enjoy delving into their deep meaning and nuances. You can use a thesaurus, but understand that each word has a slightly different twist. How is a word perceived when it is read?

You need to choose the word that is effective, rather than a synonym that is not. As Mark Twain said, the importance of choosing just the right word is the difference between lightning and lightning-bug.

Work Space

Establish a work space of your own—even if it's the corner of a kitchen table. At the very least, you'll need the following:

- A work space for your computer, typewriter, or laptop.
- Good lighting for both your computer and for your notes and research.
- A flat surface where you can spread out notes, books, and other materials.
- A place to file research notes, articles, and other information.
- A place to store supplies where they are readily accessible.
- A space for your most useful reference books.
—Moira Allen, from "Ten Steps You Can Take Today: Toward Becoming a Freelance Writer," on the Web site www.writing-world.com

Business Acumen

Writing is your business. But it is intertwined with the publishing business, and therefore so are you. It behooves you to know as much as you can learn about what happens with your writing from idea to publication, and beyond. You are putting your words, and perhaps a bit of yourself, out there whenever you submit a manuscript, or see one of your books or magazine pieces released to the world.

In Appendix B, you will find some excellent books to read on the business of writing from the publisher's perspective, as well as that of the writer.

The publishing business goes far beyond the desk of your editor. It also is shaped by the people involved in marketing, production, distribution, and bookselling. And beyond your publisher—what is happening with the competition?

You will benefit from staying current on what is happening within the publishing industry. Trade journals such as *Publishers Weekly* and *Editor & Publisher* are excellent sources of news about publishing; most libraries subscribe to one or both. National newspapers like the *Wall Street Journal* are another good source for publishing news.

You cannot become an expert on the entire publishing business. But try at least to keep up with some important news. You might discover a book or magazine editor changing jobs or a publisher starting a new magazine or a new line of books. If you hear that a publisher was gobbled up by another firm, it might help to know why—and how this will affect you and your livelihood.

The most valuable information is current market information. Who is buying what, how much of it, and what would they love to publish next? We'll talk about that in later chapters. Market information indicates the desired interim destinations on the roadmap of your writing career. Think of it as your AAA guidebook. Whether you write full-time or part-time, you need up-to-date market information. Otherwise, you'll end up in the ghost towns of non-paying publishers. Or end up at a seasonal attraction that just closed its doors and won't open again until you're long gone. You want to find the best, most enjoyable stopovers, and travel the quickest, easiest, and safest routes to get there.

You can learn quite a bit about the publishing business from other writers. Writers love to talk about publishers—who they like to work with, and who they don't. Just as other professionals network, so should you. Venues for meeting other writers include writers' conferences and workshops, national or regional trade shows, and conventions of fans of various categories of genre fiction (such as mystery, romance, or science fiction).

There are also local, regional, and national organizations for writers. Some are general in focus (the Author's Guild, for instance); others are specific-interest groups (Mystery Writers of America, American Association of Aviation Writers). Any can provide a gateway to networking. You'll get newsletters with information often not available anywhere else, including opportunities to meet your peers, as well as editors and publishers working in your field.

It's like talking with truckers at a rest stop; they know every detour and speed trap for hundreds of miles in any direction. And they love to share what they know.

Buying Success

There are some things you cannot buy—not for any amount of money.

Oddly enough, getting published is not one of those things. If you want badly enough to be published, and have a few thousand dollars to throw away, you can get your book into print. In most cases this is not a great idea, particularly if you want to see your work in bookstores and libraries around the country. It's likely you will end up with a slimmer bank balance, some boxes of self-published books stuck away in a closet, and no real demand for them.

Some writers have succeeded in self-publishing, from Benjamin Franklin to the present day. For those interested in this approach, Dan Poynter's book The Self-Publishing Manual (Para Publishing) is a good place to start. There are also a number of print-on-demand vendors, such as Xlibris, who will gladly print your book for you—if you are willing to pay for it.

But for most authors, the respectable and profitable way to get into print is to have your book acquired, edited, and published for its merit and suitability to a publisher's existing market of readers.

Professionalism

For freelance writers, professionalism can be expressed as knowing how to work with editors to meet their needs. Editors' needs usually reflect these basic concerns:

1. *Subject.* The subject matter of your work must be firmly within the publisher's area(s) of interest—in their eyes, not just in your opinion. Don't try to sell a how-to article on palmistry to *Time Magazine.* You won't find a ready buyer for a horror novel with an editor at Harlequin (the romance publisher).

2. *Current Need.* This reflects what readers are buying and what the editor anticipates will be needed in the near future.

3. *Approach.* How you approach or slant a book, article, or short story is crucial. Tom Clancy probably couldn't have sold *The Hunt for Red October* to the Naval Institute Press if it was a novel in which the Russian fleet finds Ramos and the Red October stealth submarine. Similarly, I doubt you'll find any interest in an article disproving psychic phenomena for *Fate Magazine.* Publishers, editors, and audiences have their preferences and proclivities. You need to find the right slant.

4. *Timing.* In the publishing world, timing is everything. Consider all the many articles and books that come out soon after the death of a famous person or after a major event in world history. The ideal situation is when you submit a manuscript to an editor who has been looking for something just like it—but hasn't been able to find it until you came along. On the other hand, if you try to sell a wizards-and-elves trilogy to Bantam Books when they've already saturated the market, you'll be rejected.

5. *Meeting Deadlines.* Once deadlines are set, publishers need your work on time, and in the condition and coverage they expected. One of the most important aspects for a publisher

is the ability of a writer to meet deadline with quality material. The publishing world lives and dies with its deadlines—and you will too.

Professionalism also includes keeping work as work. With my friends who are also editors, I suspend personal relationships when we talk business. I've sold to each of them, and I've been rejected by each of them, and it hasn't affected our friendships. Nor have our friendships affected the work I've done for them—I don't try to leverage anything on the basis or friendship, and neither do they.

Experience in Selling Your Work

Before you can think seriously about writing full-time, you must have an extensive list of respectable, well-paying publishing credits. This doesn't mean you have to publish eight books and 200 magazine articles before you can make a go of it. You do need enough sales in a specific area so an editor in that field will recognize that you are a serious freelancer—and will be willing to read your work and consider buying it.

With a solid, impressive list of publishing credits, you give editors some assurance that your writing will be consistent and of suitable quality. Think about it. If you were an editor, would you choose an experienced writer over an unpublished writer? Of course.

We'll talk about this much more extensively in later chapters.

Optimism

You have to keep a good attitude to write for a living. How do you regard your writing ability, your marketing acumen, and your prospects for the future?

You have to be an optimist—and radiate that even when you

Fans or Customers?
I have no fans. You know what I got? Customers.
—Mickey Spillane,
(quoted in The Write Book, edited by Bob Perlongo)

feel pessimistic for a moment or two, as we all do now and then. You must know and communicate to others that you are good enough to sell your work, that the markets will continue to support you, that you're flexible enough to take on almost any kind of writing project. Yes, the writing business has a lot of ups and downs, for writers and publishers alike. And it's full of pessimists. But the optimists do better; they get more work, deliver it faster, and bounce back faster from occasional setbacks.

Until I started writing for a living, I thought I was a pessimist. But now I know different: Without my deep-seated, ultimately cheery optimism, I'd never have made it for one year—much less 20! Late checks, impossible deadlines, canceled contracts and columns . . . all of these and more could have easily run my career right into a dead-end.

But besides being a full-time writer, I'm a full-time optimist. Even when I complain about the second edition of my best-selling book being delayed, and the IRS threatens to grab things in an unpleasant fashion just because of some paperwork gone astray, I'm planning what I'll write next to make up for it all.

You'll have to be an optimist, too. Otherwise, even though you're delighted to be your own boss, you'll start to feel the effects of the lack of guaranteed income, schedule, and the rest. If you are an optimistic freelance writer, however, the world is your oyster. There are many ways to succeed, and you know you can find one or more paths that will be right for you.

Desire to Succeed

What is desire? It lies somewhere between wanting and needing. Where exactly is that line drawn? For me, it's the place where you know you could live without something, but you want it so much that the quest for it almost becomes a reason for existence.

Think of de Soto looking for the Fountain of Youth. Or Sir Richard Francis Burton on his quest to find the headwaters of the Nile. Perhaps you know someone who was so focused on something (getting into West Point, giving birth, buying a home, winning a marathon, overcoming a handicap, or anything of similar importance) that they succeeded.

Why did they persist? Because they believed they could find what they sought; they knew in their heart that they could do whatever was needed to reach their goal.

You need to have that quality of true desire to succeed as a full-time writer. You must know that it can be done, and know that you can do it, not by cheers or chants, but by buckling down daily to write, to research information and markets, to submit, to resubmit when you get rejections in the mail, and to get published. And to keep doing it, over and over, as the publication credits mount, your income grows, and your experience matures.

Why? Because it's your heartfelt desire. Desire is a powerful stirring of the heart and spirit that is as fundamental as a law of physics. It's what causes the proverbial body in motion to move in the first place. Because it wants to go somewhere.

Motivation to Communicate

What motivates you to write? Are you looking for extra income? Or do you just wish to share what you know? Perhaps you want to do something for which others will respect you. Or maybe you have a pressing need to tell the stories that you feel need telling.

There is no correct answer to that question. You may write for any or all of those reasons. They all serve as motivations for me, along with other reasons, too. The important thing is that you have motivations, and that you recognize them.

Motivation plays a role like that of the engine of a car moving down the highway. It provides the forward propulsion. Without it, you may have all sorts of potential—and even desire—to go somewhere, but there's no purpose.

Motivations (yes, we all have more than one) give you purpose and sustain motion. If you write a story just to write any old story, there's no purpose in it. If, however, you have a theme,

Publishing Today

Publishers are always on the lookout for a good book. This is something to keep in mind no matter how discouraging the prospect of finding a publisher is, no matter how many rejection slips you get, and no matter how overwhelming the odds seem.

—Richard Balkin,
A Writer's Guide to Book Publishing, 1977

something to say, that makes you want to share your story with others, you have motivations and purpose. You are not merely writing with a pencil or tapping a keyboard; you are creating something for a reason. You wish to communicate clearly.

A writing career may start with a desire, but motivations translate that into continued action. Even people with great desire may find themselves flagging now and then. Your motivations—to succeed, to not lose face, to tell the best story you can, to do the right thing—often are what keep you going, even when the route is uphill.

Discipline to Write (and Keep Writing)

How determined are you to achieve your writing goals? Can you work around obstacles? Can you resist the temptation to spend Sunday afternoon in the park or with your favorite hobby or pastime, and instead spend that precious time writing? What about fun-to-read magazines arriving in the mail, friends and relatives coming to visit, and other daily events that threaten to take away the time you might have put into writing?

It all requires self-discipline—which I define as the techniques or means to do what you need to do, even if you don't want to do it.

Self-discipline is an odd quality. Without it, I couldn't have written this book, or any of the others I've written. For this book, for example, I had to work around a number of obstacles, from computer disasters to family emergencies. Even as I write these words, I am mightily tempted to go read a book, explore Web sites, or go out to visit someone. My daughter's birthday is today, and she's leaving for France in just two days. And I really need to take my car in for some work. And the grass in the yard needs cutting. And on and on.

But I cannot succumb to such temptations. Like many writers, I have my motivations to stay with a particular project. But motivation just keeps you moving in the general direction of where you want to go. More or less on a daily basis, I have to exercise more than a little self-discipline to keep from giving in to all the distracting temptations I have at the moment.

In my journey as a writer, self-discipline keeps me from getting distracted by too many fun (but potentially too costly in time or money) things I spy—ice cream stands, cactus-jelly huts, intriguing ghost towns, and so on. It's also what keeps me attentive to the small things: I've got a tankful of gas, the oil's been changed, and the sun roof isn't leaking. The engine won't die at the first sign of extreme heat or cold.

I have somewhere to go—and once I get rolling, I enjoy the smooth-running, efficient vehicle that's taking me there.

So, how's your self-discipline? Are you naturally a procrastinator? (I am, too; most writers are.) If so, you need self-discipline more than the average human.

I'll offer tips on how to tune up all these inner qualities—especially your self-discipline—later in this book. They are essential to make your journey successful.

Remember, too, that the journey should be as enjoyable as reaching your destination. So always keep those inner qualities, especially your desire and motivations, right out in the open. The more you understand and focus on what drives you to be a full-time freelance writer, the more likely you will succeed.

On Discipline

There is no way to success in art but to take off your coat . . . and work like a digger on the railroad, all day and every day.

—Ralph Waldo Emerson

CHAPTER 2

What It's Really Like

YOU'VE SEEN A BIT OF FULL-TIME WRITING from the outside. This chapter shows you what it's like on the inside—living and working as a full-time writer. Remember: as a freelance writer, you control nearly everything to do with work. (That's "nearly.") That includes when and where you work, and how you work.

My Schedule Is My Own

As I write this, it's 8:00 p.m. on a Thursday. I took off this morning to go to an auction. I collect fairly odd stuff, and I particularly enjoy weekday auctions because there's less competition. Many regular weekend bidders can't take off work during the week.

Of course, to make that up, I'm working for a couple of hours this evening, because at the moment this book is my top-priority writing assignment.

Similarly, if there's a wedding, a family emergency, any sort of weekday appointment, I have no problem getting some time away from work. The same holds true for evenings and weekends.

And now and then, I take off a day or two to recharge. Of course, like the hours spent here and there, I usually find a way to make up that rest time by working into the evenings or weekends later, especially when faced with an imminent deadline.

I found such things very difficult to do when I worked for someone else. For anything other than a family funeral, or child in the hospital, my immediate supervisors suddenly found that I was indispensable to the company. Right!

When I worked for someone else, I lost money if I took off. In freelancing, you don't lose anything except the time—as long as you complete the assignments or work for which you've contracted. And there are no negative consequences to arranging your schedule to fit your personal needs.

And for me, there's another benefit: Unlike when I worked a regular day job, now I can get all the sleep I need. I just often work a little later into the day.

Work at Home!

I always laugh a bit when I see the work-at-home cons that show up in small ads in the backs of magazines (just as they have for 80 years, and more) and now via the Internet. I devoted about 20,000 words to the topic of such scams in another book, *Web Psychos, Stalkers, and Pranksters*—which explained what some of the most common offers are, and how the person offering it makes money, while you don't. Yes, there are cons out there aimed at writers looking for work. Just remember this: If it sounds too good to be true, it is.

However, in many ways, freelance writing is indeed the ideal work-at-home occupation. You don't need a lot of fancy machinery or special equipment, there's no inventory to store, and you don't need a license. You don't create pollution. You use things that you would probably own, anyway—a computer and an Internet connection. Oh, you might make more trips to the post office, or the FedEx driver might stop at your house more often, but aside from that there's no real indication to the outside world that you're working at all.

Not only can you work at home, you can work wherever you want in your home. In fact, you can work anywhere you can take a laptop or palmtop computer (or a typewriter), or even a pencil and pad of paper. If you really want to, you can even work when you're traveling on vacation.

I've been working wherever I wished for years. I have a laptop computer that's allowed me to write out on the backyard deck, in the living room—wherever. I've also often used it to write on the road and sometimes, when the fancy strikes, in a beautiful park about a mile from my home.

If you are still working at a regular job—even if your tasks lend themselves to it—try getting a supervisor to let you work at a nice park up the street. No way! They want to be able to "see" that you're working, because they don't trust you. And then what about the other employees?—they'll demand to work off-site, too. Despite the growing popularity of telecommuting, you generally can't get out of the factory, office, or shop unless it clearly saves the company plenty of money, or creates greater efficiency.

One great benefit: no commuting! That saves time and resources, and eliminates a major source of stress.

And then there's the lack of demands on my wardrobe. Consider the companies where you've been employed. Could you have worked in your underwear or robe? Lying on the floor? How about taking your baby to work? Or your dog? Odds are you could never do such things "at work," not even at those

The Writer's Study

The fantasy of a cozy writing studio crammed with books and other beloved objets can be taken too far. Writers who festoon the workplace with a lifetime's mementos may never write again. They will daydream and pace the study like a high-brow television host, fondling books and glass paperweights and murmuring poignant opening lines such as, "How swiftly passed the days . . ."

Many a writer has dissipated the creative force in fashioning bookshelves, sanding furniture, and equipping the perfect study—which then sits idle. . . . The best writing room may be the most mundane, not a study at all, but a small office with ample desk and work tools suggesting a day's labor.

—Arthur Plotnik, in The Elements of Authorship, 2000

progressive companies that claim to accommodate all the needs of their employees.

As a freelance writer, I wear shorts, or jeans, and a T-shirt most of the time. Sophie the Dog doesn't mind a bit. Nor does she mind my taste in music; if it's disagreeable, she goes into another room.

My work environment is never too cold or too hot. The thermostat is set wherever I like it to be. I take breaks whenever I wish. You don't have to waste time or effort "accommodating" others in the workplace. You are in control of your environment, and that's more than a little relaxing.

Making the leap to full-time writing offers many benefits to your personal life. If you have small children and have in the past been the one who went off to work, you'll now discover that you can take a greater part in their lives. You'll also find that you're often a hit with your partner or spouse, because you have more time to take care of your household responsibilities.

But It's Not a Vacation

Writing full-time and being in charge of your days can be a nice life most of the time. But it's not a vacation. While you may choose to work when, where, and how you wish, you do work. Lots.

In fact, you are likely to work more hours than you would at a full-time job. The majority of full-timers I've talked with agree that they work more hours writing as freelancers than they ever did for an employer. Personally, I average 54 hours per week.

Actually, you may find that you want to work more hours. Why? For any of several reasons:

- *It doesn't feel like "work."* This is my favorite reason. Even after 20 years at this, writing doesn't feel like work. (Sometimes I would rather be doing something else, though.)

- *A strong desire to succeed and convince others that you are working and busy as a writer.* This is me, too. Consequently, I am the hardest person to work for I know. I require more of myself than any foreman or manager ever did.

- *Preparing for dry spells.* There are dry spells in any writing career. So the prudent writer often takes on more projects than necessary, to prepare for times when business is slow and income drops.

- *Too many ideas.* It's safe to say that all of us have more ideas than we could ever turn into books or magazine pieces—or anything else. So, whenever we have the time, we eagerly pull out that pet project that we always wanted to see get into print.

- *A feeling of responsibility.* Here again, this spurs me. I accept my failures and successes, and can see the direct relationship between how much I work and how much I accomplish and earn. More than anything else, this gives me a feeling of power, knowing I control what I do.

- *Owning the company.* Finally, there's the fact that we own the company, so to speak. Look at anyone who owns any small business; they're putting in whatever hours it takes to succeed, taking pride in seeing their name on the product or service they provide.

At times, of course, you have to work many more hours than you wish. Especially when you find yourself against a deadline. Like any small business you depend on your customers or clients for your income. Hence, you sometimes have to work longer or harder than you might choose, to accommodate clients.

A freelancer's clients are mostly editors. And editors have deadlines. You must meet those deadlines, even if it means missing the family reunion, a Woodstock reunion, your favorite TV show, or whatever. All sorts of things can come up to throw you off a deadline. You have to be willing to work around these road-blocks, or your writing career will go nowhere. (On the positive side, when you do make a difficult deadline, you can often take some time off—and you have an editor who is willing to do business with you again.)

Running in Place?

Remember the scene in *Alice in Wonderland*, when the Red Queen says to Alice, ". . . it takes all the running you can do, to keep in the same place. If you want to get somewhere else, you must run at least twice as fast as that!"

Writing for a living can be like that sometimes.

Why? Because, while I've talked about control of your work, a writing career involves many things over which you have no control. Every day, arbitrary decisions that can affect you and your work are made by people you may never even have heard of. A magazine's budget for freelance work might be reduced, because key advertisers have canceled long-term commitments. A line of books might be killed, or altered to accommodate what is selling best for a publisher—which happens to be projects that you aren't working on.

The results sometimes hit hard, or sometimes just trickle down. Maybe the magazine editor can't pay as much as he or she would like. Of course, you could end up with more work, because other writers refuse to accept the new pay scales, and have ready markets elsewhere. Or you may find that you need the money at the time, and don't have other places to turn to. In that case, your best response is to take what's offered, and quietly look around for a new market. Your loyalty could pay off, with more work at higher pay if the magazine recovers. If not, you've begun to diversify your sources of income in case the magazine fails.

Likewise, if your book publisher folds a line that includes your book or books, or goes under entirely, you will find yourself desperately seeking a new publisher for your next book—unless you are prepared for such an eventuality.

How do you prepare? Cultivate acquaintances with editors and with other writers. It doesn't hurt to be on a friendly basis with an editor at a different publisher. That person may remember you if another writer fails to turn in a book manuscript. Or your name may come up when he or she is looking for just the right person to do a manuscript or proposal review.

All of this may look like running in place. Try to stay on top of events in the publishing world, and build contacts with editors and writers. This may not yield anything beyond some delightful friendships, but for me, this is reason enough.

Dealing with Ups & Downs

Money is an extremely important element of writers' lives. Unexpected situations can turn a writer's world inside out. Here are a couple of examples from my own career.

In 1990, I was invited to write a column for a new magazine called *Windows*. It was a grand publication, the biggest and most popular in its field. The Editor, Fred Langa, had left another prestigious magazine in the computer industry *(Byte),* to edit *Winmag*, as we called it.

Fred asked me to write the column. It was a wonderful job, and paid $1,000 per month, for only about 10 hours' work. In today's dollars, that would be near $2,000. And I was listed as a Contributing Editor on the magazine's masthead.

Eighteen months later, I had a call from one of the department editors. He told me the publisher had canceled my column. Why? Because there were so few advertisers in the area I was covering.

Wham! More than 5 percent of my income just disappeared. But I wasn't unprepared. I immediately contacted the editor of a smaller magazine, and made a deal for a column that, while it

A Gamble
The profession of book-writing makes horse racing seem like a solid, stable business.
—John Steinbeck

Money Does Matter!

For a freelance writer, money is more than just a way to pay the bills; it's a motivational tool as well. Why? First, the publishers you work with are in the business to make money. They ask their customers to pay their own hard-earned money to be able to read your writing. So both customers and publishers need to think your words are worthy enough to shell out some cash for them.

To think like a publisher—to slant your writing to be valuable to your audience of readers—always ask yourself: Would I pay good money to read what I've written?

Second, nearly all of your competitors (other writers in the field) are also thinking this way. Including yours truly. So you need to write something good enough to beat out the rest of us if you want to sell your work to a given market.

Money helps calculate the relative value of your writing. If an editor at Havoc House Publishers offers you an advance of $8,000 for your novel, but gives me a $15,000 advance, who does the publisher see as the more valuable writer?

Even if you live on a trust fund, just won the lottery, or are entirely supported by someone else, money is a means of keeping score.

It's a way to measure your progress, to spur you to improve your writing, and to evaluate how valuable your work is to others.

paid only $150 per month, took less time, and kept me in print regularly.

I've experienced other drastic setbacks. One of my publishers simply ceased to exist. It was doing fine five years earlier, when I wrote a book for the company. But its parent company decided it wasn't earning enough profit.

Two more book publishers canceled my contracts in the wake of the attacks of September 11, 2001. When the economy suddenly slowed down, their sales dropped as much as 70 percent. Both involved lines of computer books, an industry hit hard by the economic drop.

I wasn't the only writer who lost money. Hundreds of other writers saw their contracts canceled as well. For me, $25,000 in expected income over an immediate four-month period just disappeared from my budget.

The moral? Just because you can't imagine something, doesn't mean it won't happen.

So Be Prepared!

The best way to prepare for unforeseen events is to have more than one project going at a time. That way, you'll not be completely crippled if fate comes down hard on your career. Personally, I try to have a book contract and two or more magazine article assignments (and perhaps a short story) underway at any one time.

This advice is of vital importance to full-time writers. Besides spreading the load income-wise, you also get a psychological break of sorts. With two projects working at once, you have less emotion at risk if one of the projects turns a little bumpy.

And remember to save up cash to help you weather the storms of fate. With that buffer between you and homelessness, if markets suddenly dry up, you can spend some time and turn to writing something new, rather than worrying about money.

The Writing Life

If I had to describe an ideal life for a writer, it would be something like this: more than enough money, the best computer system available, a very large house on a peaceful five acres (with a dog door for Sophie the Dog), and lots of fan letters.

Hmm . . . add a tolerant partner or spouse, and a nice climate with an ocean nearby. Plus, there are a few other things that would be ideal, but there's no room to list them here. (Feel free to guess how much I have of what I've described.)

Oh—and don't forget: a publisher who thinks I'm a best-selling genius, and spends the money on promotion to make it true.

There is no absolute to aim for in your writing career. Still, I can give you an idea of how some of us full-time writers work.

The Typical Situation

Mostly, full-time writers have the same kinds of lives as you, your friends and family, or other people you know. Much of their lives are centered around the sorts of things that are important to anyone: relatives, marriages or other relationships, home, hobbies, maybe children and pets, travel, and so on.

My own life as a writer is a bit odd, and a bit normal. I have a grown daughter and son whom I love very much. When my children were in grade school and high school, I helped out by speaking to classes, being a "Computer Dad" and a band parent. I was also a scout leader. A couple of times in the late 1980s I got involved in party politics. (Yes—the smoke-filled back rooms still exist!)

I've owned a couple of houses, but now rent. I've lived alone, and not alone. I have pets. I like stylish cars and pickup trucks. My hobbies usually involve collecting something. And I have way too many books.

So far, there's little to distinguish me from any number of my neighbors in the upper-middle-class neighborhood of the college town where I live.

Oh, I have a beard and sometimes longish hair—not because I'm a writer, but probably because I'm stuck culturally in 1967.

Only if you start watching my daily routines, though, will you notice some real differences from my neighbors. I'm at home a lot during the day. I never go to work. I seem to stay up late, and sleep in most mornings.

I spend an inordinate amount of time at the keyboard—even more than people hooked on Internet chat rooms. And I run short of cash more often than most folks (usually around tax time).

Too, I sometimes disappear for days, for no apparent reason. (The reasons are simple: I take mini-vacations, and get invited to speak at a lot of writers' conferences and similar gatherings.) Sometimes people see my face on television or in the local newspapers, commenting on something in my fields of special interest.

That's it. That's me. That's my life as a writer, in a nutshell. Things that happen to me or around me are the same sorts of things that happen to people no matter what their job.

In sum, I lead a fairly typical life. So do nearly all of the full-time writers I know. They have mortgages, annoying relatives, a home, car, and so forth. Some have more money than others. Some are real jerks, but most are among the nicest people you'd want to meet. More or less, we mirror the demographic makeup of the U.S.

Even the super-wealthy writers are often cut from the same cloth. Stephen King has a grand home and suffers the celebrity malaise of being known wherever he goes. If you get a chance to talk with him, though, you'll discover he's much like any other writer. The first time I met him, in 1983, we griped about publishers and talked about dogs.

My late friend Martin Caidin (creator of the *Six Million Dollar Man,* and author of more than 100 books) was a different story. If you had been this man's neighbor, you would see immediately that he was very different. He was a stocky, no-neck bull of a man, with shaved head and giant handlebar moustaches, usually wearing blue jeans and a leather jacket, with an attitude to match.

If you've read any of his novels, you may know more about him than you realize; much of his writing used people, events, and places from his own life. The man lived several lives in the span of one. He'd run covert operations in South America, spent time in occupied Japan interrogating war prisoners, and owned a bunch of war birds (WWII fighter and bomber aircraft). And that's not even scratching the surface.

Writing was just one of his passions. He'd drop out of sight now and then to write a book, then go right back to flying and other things. He wrote adventure and science fiction novels, and books about World War II fighter aces and their airplanes.

And yes, Marty and I griped about publishers a lot—and talked about dogs.

It's a Wonderful Life

So, what's it gonna be? A mansion in the Hamptons? An apartment in Taos? A painted-lady Victorian home in San Francisco?

Or a modest home in a small college town in Ohio?

Wherever you live and write, you'll be mostly just like everyone else around you. Yes, you'll work at home and have a little more control over some circumstances of your daily life, especially schedules and workplace settings. But in most respects, writers are just like everyone else in our communities, except that we work at home.

And that's a good choice—for a lot of reasons.

Financially, the choices are yours, too. What kind of lifestyle will your income allow? Will it be food stamps or filet mignon? Welfare or royalties?

The next chapter will get you going on your way to organizing your workplace, and managing it like a successful business.

CHAPTER 3

Self-Management Tools for the Writer

I HAVE FRIENDS WHO WOULD SNICKER at the thought of me writing about how to get organized. To those who visit my home office, I may appear to be the most disorganized person to have ever turned to writing as a living.

Yet, even though the surface of my desk is completely covered by books, papers, and some things you wouldn't believe, there is order in the midst of it. It's just not evident at a glance.

Organization is required to keep control over projects. It's also a way to help yourself focus on writing, rather than on getting to your writing.

Organizing Your Writing Projects

There are hundreds of tools to help you get organized. Visit any office supply store, and you'll find things you didn't know existed, along with lots of things you do know well: filing cabinets, magazine holders, bookshelves, file boxes, dividers, labels, diaries, calendars, and on and on.

I'm not going to recommend that you use this item or that. On the continuum between orderly and organic, there are an infinite number of points. What you choose to use depends on how you organize. You can create very elaborate systems; some people need them to feel professional and organized. Others get by with an amorphous system that no one else can understand. That's what I do.

Compartmentalization & Accessibility

All organization is essentially compartmentalization and accessibility. That is, everything for a given project is kept separate from anything else, and it is stored in a location and in such a way as to make it immediately accessible.

This is the best summary I can give you of how to get your projects organized.

Personally, I do not have what it takes to get organized like a business or government agency. I am always either highly focused on a project, or easily distracted.

When I am focused, I have a tendency to forget what I'm supposed to do with an item when I've finished with it. The danger is that I will put things down on any flat surface, so I can go back to what I was doing. When I do that, things get covered up by other things, and I forget what I put where.

If I had an elaborate filing system, however, taking the time to develop and use it would distract me from my writing. For me, keeping up with a complicated filing system would waste as much time as misplacing something. Plus, I have no patience for dealing with any sort of filing system that is too complicated. For me, the simpler, the better.

Knowing that, I have devised over the years a system to protect myself from my tendency to be disorganized. I had to come up with this in self-defense. If I hadn't, the amount of time it would have taken me to find things would have been a major barrier to my writing success.

How I Organize

Everything that has to do with my writing is compartmentalized, beginning with stacks of paper on my desk. Although these look like a terrible mess, each is composed of related papers. At the moment, the main pile consists of edited manuscript pages for this book. Another has ingoing and outgoing letters and bills.

The key to all of this is that each pile contains things (mostly paper) related to a specific current project. When I'm finished with these two piles, what is left is put away on a large shelf, stored in magazine holders (cardboard or plastic containers that keep magazines upright, with a cutaway profile on each side and in front so you can remove a magazine or other item easily). This allows me to eyeball quickly what is in each holder, and to visually keep track of the volume.

Within each magazine holder, typically, are folders—in no specific order—stuffed with related papers, books, photos, and magazines.

When I no longer need them no longer—when the project is completed—the materials in the magazine holders are either stored, reshelved (in the case of books), or trashed.

An obvious and highly visual mode of organization, this method has a special appeal for me because I don't have to think too much or remember anything complicated to find an item. I just know which holder an item is in. Also, when I am finished handling a

Letterhead

Develop a simple, professional letterhead. It should include your name, address, and phone number (and you may also wish to include a fax number and e-mail address).

The least expensive way to develop stationery is to design it on your computer, using a large, readable font. (Some people like to put a dividing line between the letterhead and the body of the letter.)

Avoid "cute" logos like pens or parchments, and don't give yourself a "title" such as "author" or "writer at large."

You can save the letterhead as a file, or have it printed at a local print shop.

It's not a bad idea to use a better-quality paper for your query and cover letters than for your manuscripts—a linen or parchment stock in a neutral color such as ivory or gray works well.

—Moira Allen, from "Ten Steps You Can Take Today: Toward Becoming a Freelance Writer," on the Web site www.writing-world.com

piece of paper or magazine or whatever, I don't put off storing it. It is just as easy to stuff quickly it into one of the folders as it is to find a more permanent spot to place it.

It takes almost no time. I don't have to look for anything (the magazine holders are large), and I don't worry about putting something in the exact spot from which it came.

You may prefer a more traditional filing cabinet system. But for me, the problem with filing cabinets is that they don't allow me to associate batches of files, magazines, and other diverse materials as freely as I can with the magazine holders. For my creative work, I like to throw lots of things into proximity, kept close at hand, to sort and review as needed. For me, filing cabinet systems are too rigid. I like to organize my papers by projects, because that's how my work needs are organized.

I also organize based on priority. Whatever I'm currently working on is easiest to find. Material for this book, for instance, is in two large magazine holders next to a big lamp on a table by my desk. I look in that direction at least 50 times a day when I'm at my desk. Material for a couple of other books I'd like to write, and for magazine articles I'll be working on when this book is complete, are lined up on the shelves of a big bookcase.

Just to make sure I'm not missing anything, I sort out and reorganize folders and their contents every six weeks or so. After that, it's all downhill for a month or so, until the next spurt of cleanup.

In the interim, though, so long as I don't let the magazine folders migrate out of sight, I'm in good shape. I know I can rely on my short-term memory to keep track of what is in each project collection, which is the real index to this filing system. My system is fluid, ever-evolving, and right at my fingertips. It works for me.

That's the secret. However you organize, it must work well for you. A freelance writer needs to be efficient. You aren't being paid to maintain your files. You are being paid to produce sellable pieces of writing.

Anyone can get organized. All you need do is compartmentalize and make sure everything is easily accessible.

Keeping Business Records

When it comes to keeping paperwork relating to your financial payments, contracts, correspondence worth saving, and other important business records, you do need to be more organized. These records are not accessed as frequently as project material. This means you cannot rely on short-term memory to tell you into which box or folder you may have slipped a check stub or receipt. But when you need such things, you usually need them quickly. That requires better organization. However, this is relatively simple, as these types of records fit into traditional filing cabinets or file boxes more easily. They are more uniform, are easily organized by vendor, project, or calendar month, and usually fit into envelopes or file folders very nicely.

As a full-time freelancer, you will have more record-keeping to do than you did as a part-time writer. You'll need to keep more receipts, contracts, check stubs and vouchers, correspondence, research notes, and other such paperwork. This is all the more reason to organize these records methodically.

I use basically the same approach as I use to keep my household records. For regular business transactions, I put each month's expense receipts into a large envelope; these go into a file box with dividers labeled by month. Check stubs go into the same box, in envelopes separate from the receipts. This allows me to pull them all out at tax time to total the year's activity.

I keep all contracts together in one place. You can file these important documents by date or in alphabetical order, by name of the publication.

If you submit invoices, keep unpaid ones in a separate folder, so you can find the paperwork when a payment is made—or send a reminder if payment is late. Be sure to make two copies of each invoice: one to submit and one for your files.

Woes of a Writer
I love being a writer. What I can't stand is the paperwork.
—Peter De Vries

Tracking Manuscripts and Submissions

It is an understatement to say that keeping track of where you send your manuscripts and what happens to them is important. With a properly kept submission record, you can check to see whether a manuscript or query has been outstanding too long without a reply. When should you start to expect a reply, and when do you need to follow up to inquire about a submission? In addition, the record will help you avoid a faux pas such as submitting a manuscript twice to the same publisher, or submitting a manuscript you've already sold.

For years—even after I got my first computer—I kept paper records of my submissions. They're easy and fast to access. All you need is a one-sheet form that looks something like the grid and box setup in Figure 3-1.

Title	Magazine	Date	Reject Accept	Amount Received	Payment Date	Type
Phone Call from Mars	Analog SF	11/13/04	Accepted	$235.20	12/22/04	S
Secret Searches	PC World	8/8/04	Accepted	$1,500.00	4/17/05	A
The Future Reconsidered	Atlantic Monthly	9/14/04	Rejected	$0.00		A
The Henry Ford of Radio	Smithsonian	10/28/04	Accepted	$2,000.00	1/12/05	A
Using Photo Archives for Research	Online Librarian	11/22/04	Accepted	$150.00	2/18/05	A
Wounded and Walking Fast	Analog SF	11/2/04	Rejected	$0.00		S

Figure 3-1. Simple manuscript tracking form

Make the headers whatever you like, then fill the rest of a sheet of paper with the same empty boxes, print it out, and make new copies as needed. (This was done in less than one minute with Microsoft Word's Table feature.)

If you want to be really detailed and precise, fire up Excel or any other spreadsheet program, and create something like this:

Title	Submitted to	Date	Reject Accept	Payment Amount	Payment Date	Type	
Wounded and Walking Fast	Analog SF	11/2/02	Rejected	$0.00		S	
The Henry Ford of Radio	Smithsonian	11/28/02	Accepted	$2,000.00	1/12/03	A	
A Castle to Call Home	Grit	9/6/04	Accepted	$250.00	2/28/05	A	
Review: A Dearth of Time	Locus	9/14/04	Accepted	$150.00	11/21/04	R	
Secret Searches	PC World	10/8/04	Accepted	$1,500.00	4/17/05	A	
The Future Reconsidered	Atlantic Monthly	10/14/04	Rejected			A	

Figure 3-2. A spreadsheet-based manuscript tracking form

That way, you can search and sort on criteria, like all the manuscripts submitted to a certain magazine.

Or you can just keep a notebook or a word file, and write or type all relevant information.

Use whatever you feel comfortable using. But remember: you have to keep this submission log up-to-date. Also, information in this record may be needed for other purposes, such as income tax audits, banking records, or your own analysis of your productivity. Selling work is important, but submitting it steadily—and keeping accurate records of that process—is just as crucial.

Managing Your Time

As noted, one big advantage to writing full-time is the ability to work at your own schedule. Whether you're a morning person or a night person, you can work when you feel your best.

However, this isn't a constant. If you need to do research, conduct interviews, or take photos, you will probably have to break out of your preferred pattern. The same is true when you must meet a deadline. And, of course, on occasion personal matters may have to get worked into your work schedule.

For instance, I am not a morning person; I do my best work in the late afternoons and evenings. However, I can work in the mornings, or can be somewhere at eight in the morning to get an interview, if need be. I've also come up against hard deadlines where I had to work all waking hours to complete the project.

You will most likely come up against similar obstacles. This is why you need to be able to organize and control your time to make the best use of it.

Identify the best time of day (and best days of the week) to write, and do as much as possible to organize everything else around your primary targets of time to write.

Time-Management Tools

If you're already organized—perhaps you're using a Daytimer, Dayrunner, or similar scheduling tool, or have your life in your palmtop computer—that's a good start. But I have the same problems using such organizers that perhaps you do. I forget to use or postpone using the organizer, or updating it regularly.

The same is true of using a task-scheduler with an alarm, or a calendar-type scheduler, on my PC. I suspect I just feel more comfortable with something I can touch and see immediately. After all, if my PC's hard-drive crashes, how can I get at the scheduler?

So, how best to organize your time? I find a calendar with large spaces to write in to be the simplest approach. Whether it's a desktop blotter type or one that hangs on the wall, for me it's the perfect solution. It's easy to access, and you won't forget to use it—because it's always in front of you.

A pocket notebook serves well, too. And there are plenty of other tools, which you can find by browsing online or at an office-supply store. Pick what appeals to you, but whatever you choose, make it easy to find and convenient to use.

Track Your Patterns

At one point not long ago, I could tell you what work I did on any given day, because I was keeping a daily record in a large diary. In this case, the diary, designed especially for writers, was an oversized hardcover, with three dates on each page. For each date, it provided eight or ten lines on which to record appointments, activities, or work tasks completed.

I needed this tool to keep track of time I spent on a freelance contract job for the U.S. Air Force. I hadn't kept such detailed records of time spent in the past, but since I

"We'll Get Right Back to You."

No writer enjoys waiting for a response to a submission. But circumstances—vacation time, or an unusually heavy load of submissions—can cause extra delay before an editor can reply.

On the other hand, many months of waiting isn't fair to the writer. My own policy now is to allow a manuscript to linger no more than two months before I withdraw it from consideration.

There was a time when I just waited until I heard something. Like most new writers, I feared drawing a negative response by inquiring too soon or too often.

I've long since lost that particular fear.

I set my two-month limit (which is generous) after a long wait for a response from an editor who had asked to see a specific book proposal. I had happily sent in a "partial" (outline, formal proposal, and four completed chapters), confident that this would be the next book I would write.

Was I wrong! A month later, I telephoned and was told by an assistant that the editors were awash in a sea of submissions. But my partial was close to the top of the "to be read" stack.

At two months, I called again. Same message, now from another person.

I gave up calling. Instead, I wrote notes of inquiry every three or four weeks. Some were ignored; others drew apologies, with promises to look at the manuscript "very soon."

The proposal package was finally returned—rejected—six months after I had submitted it, without explanation.

However, this personal-record delay pales in comparison to one writer I know who waited 20 months for a response to a novel submission.

was doing it anyhow, I also made notes about anything else I did that involved writing or other personal tasks and pursuits.

I ended up with a remarkably concise record of work stretching over several years. The benefit: I was able to analyze how I spent my time. I was able to see a glance:

- how much time I spent writing

- my most productive hours

- the average time I was able to spend writing without interruption

- my best days for writing

- what sort of interruptions occurred most frequently

- certain expenses, such as car mileage, that I logged in the margins.

Based on all this information, I got a good handle on managing my time. I got better at predicting a certain number of unavoidable interruptions, but also learned how to avoid others. I began to see the patterns: when I naturally worked best—and when I needed to set more formal goals to do certain tasks that otherwise I tended to dodge as long as possible.

Further, as I looked back at the record, I realized I was being productive even during what felt at the time like long dry spells when no new assignments came, and little money came in. I was still busy and productive doing the work of negotiating contracts, seeking assignments, and doing market research. Every day seemed to serve a purpose; I could see the patterns of being a productive writer.

Tracking Major Projects

Are you familiar with the basics of project management? For writers, simple project management is a means of keeping track of your progress in writing a book or any other work. Project management tells you how far along you ought to be, and helps make sure you meet the project's deadline.

There are sophisticated software tools for project management. But you don't need a special program to set up effective project management for a book or article. All you really need is a calendar or file on which to write your estimates for each phase of a given project.

For example, you may be writing a book that is due on November 30. It's May 12, the book has 14 chapters, and you have some research to do. With that information, make estimates of the time it will take you to do the necessary research and write each chapter.

Once you have these estimates, create a chart with a goal date for each element (research, writing each chapter, and so on). I've put together a simulated project management chart in Figure 3-3.

Chapter Number	Progress	1	2	3	4	5	6	7	8	9	10	11	12	13	14	15	16	17	18
Chapter 1	Goal	▓																	
	Actual	X																	
Chapter 2	Goal		▓																
	Actual	X	X																
Chapter 3	Goal				▓	▓													
	Actual			X	X	X	X												
Chapter 4	Goal						▓	▓											
	Actual						X	X											
Chapter 5	Goal									▓									
	Actual									X	X								
Chapter 6	Goal											▓							
	Actual													X	X				
Chapter 7	Goal												▓	▓					
	Actual															X	X		
Chapter 8	Goal															▓	▓		
	Actual																	X	X

Figure 3-3. Simplified project management chart

Mark your completion of each stage as you go. The chart gives you a visible record of your progress. It also highlights elements of the project that are taking more time than they should.

Publishers sometimes request that you provide a similar schedule for your work on a book. The more formal and specific a deadline or goal is to you (or in almost all cases of contracted work, to your publisher), the more crucial it is to create an especially good chart. You will find that it becomes one of your most valuable self-management tools.

Dealing with Deadlines

The best advice I can give you on deadlines is: "Don't miss one." They exist for a reason. Magazine editors have to have all their advertising and editorial content finished and in their hand (including your story or article) by a certain date each month, so they can have all editing, layout work, and final proofing done so it all can be sent to their printer by another very specific and inflexible deadline.

If they do not receive your article by its deadline, they will not be happy. Turn it in early, and you will not only become a more valuable author in their eyes, you will often benefit from getting more of their time—they will have the time to read your work carefully and make extra editorial suggestions that can improve your article.

In book publishing, your deadline is there because your editor needs the manuscript and ancillary materials many months in advance in order to publish your book by a given date (pre-announced in a catalog sent to major buyers). Miss your deadline, and you may miss valuable marketing that was timed to present your work at its best. Some book publishers are on a very strict schedule, and some aren't. Either way, a lot of advance planning and resource allocation is put into play around your book manuscript. If you fall behind, you leave marketing people in the lurch; they will become disgruntled if ads are placed and run and the product isn't ready to sell and ship.

The length of time you get to complete a project varies quite a bit. In the magazine world, you may get three months—or you may be asked in an emergency to turn in a completed manuscript in two weeks. The latter happens if another author didn't meet a deadline, and the editor has empty space that must be filled. If you can produce good work quickly, you may be asked to help. (This is a good time to brush up and recycle an existing article, perhaps one that can be given a new slant for a different market.)

Book deadlines may give you as much as a year to complete a book. This is common for novels. More often, though, for nonfiction manuscripts, you get six months. Some specialized publishers (such as computer book publishers) want their manuscripts turned in within three months. That's tight, but it can be done.

On rare occasions involving time-sensitive events (like Elvis Presley's death), certain publishers will go all-out to get a book on the subject in just a few weeks.

Have I missed deadlines? Well . . . yes. Four books out of more than 40 have been completed and turned in late. As for magazines, I've been late with only two articles out of several thousand.

Planning Your Work Load

How much work is too much?

This is a tough question. To mitigate the matter of "feast or famine" for the full-time freelancer, it may be prudent to take on more work than you otherwise might ideally want to accept. Sometimes, you're working on one project, and another particularly good opportunity comes. Especially if you've

Cut-Chop: Deadline!

The Japanese have an interesting word for deadline: shimekiri. Literally translated, the word means "cut-chop." And sometimes we feel like this is not just something that we do to the work itself when up against a deadline, but something that happens to us personally.

For instance, I once received an e-mail from an editor of a Japanese magazine inquiring about the status of a column I owed him. In the message, he referred to the fact that he himself was being ". . . attacked by terrible deadlines."

At one time or another, we all feel that way.

At the time, I myself was working under many deadlines. But I didn't feel under stress, because all the pending articles and books I was working on were works I wanted to write, not assignments or contracts taken on for the money only. Which says quite a bit about deadlines, underscoring the value of writing what you enjoy.

You won't fear the attack of the "cut-chop" monsters quite as much.

just experienced a really slim period, you may feel compelled to take on more work than normal, just in case.

You are the only person who knows what your upper limit is. I type at 60 words per minute, and I know it takes about 500 hours for me to write a 400-page book, including research time. Working out the math, it appears that I could, in theory, write four or five nonfiction books in a year's time.

But I don't write just books. As we will discuss later, a full-time writing career seems to me to work best with a combination of short-term income (magazine articles, columns, etc.) and long-term, deferred income (books). So for me, the 500 hours spent writing a book are usually spread out over a few months—rather than a linear 10 or 16 weeks.

I suspect I'm typical in my productivity. I can write two or three books per year, and turn out 30 to 40 magazine columns and/or articles (some of them short). If the per-item income is fairly good, I usually set a target of writing two books, and maybe 20 articles, per year.

That puts me squarely in the middle of a range of writerly production. At one end of the scale, there are writers who can turn out a porno novel or a low-grade genre fiction novel in three ten-hour days. They tend to be demon typists, and tell pretty much the same story each time. And although these projects can provide a limited income, royalties are normally not part of such deals.

I've seen a few other good writers work equally fast. Jack Nimersheim, a friend who used to write computer books, once astounded me by writing a computer book in one week. Michael Crichton is said to write fast enough to finish a new novel in six weeks.

At the other end of the scale are novelists who take anywhere from ten months to two years to complete a novel. Some sell well, some don't. What these novelists have in common is meticulous attention to their writing and editing. They often have perfectionist tendencies—sometimes founded, I think, in a fear of failure (what I sometimes call "writer's stage fright").

If you don't already know, you'll soon figure out how much time it takes you to write a book or any shorter project. If you do already know from your records how many hours you spend on a typical writing project, extrapolate how much more you could do if you worked full-time at writing. Then . . . cut that figure by a third.

Why? Blame it on Cheops' Law, which is paraphrased as "Everything takes longer and costs more." (Cheops was the builder of one of the largest of the great pyramids in Egypt. His project ended up taking decades—a lot longer than anyone, even Cheops, had figured.)

I can almost guarantee you that any purely extrapolated calculation of how long a writing project takes will be too short, if you take just your first estimate. Why? Because there are so many things involved in writing that aren't under your direct control, and don't show up on your project records. These include, but aren't limited to:

- time spent in getting ready to do something, in putting things away, in travel to and from research sites (even if your library is right across the street)

- changes you want to make

- changes your editor requests

- outside interruptions (family, friends, pets)

- unforeseen medical problems (ever lose a day to a migraine or sinus headache?)

- accidents, power outages, equipment breakdown

It happened to Cheops and it will happen to you. Things take longer. Always factor in a goodly percentage of additional time you will spend in dealing with the unforeseen, and you won't have to watch a deadline go by because you underestimated the time you needed.

Just Say No?

When you do have to turn down work (hopefully a rare situation), try to help the editor by coming up with an alternative solution.

Ask whether you can pick up the assignment or contract later, when you have more time. Or if you have some unpublished work on hand that's appropriate, offer that (or a reprint of a published article for which you retained the rights).

Or help to find someone else to take on the job. If this works out, the author will likely return the favor in the future.

I've done all of the above. In each case, the editor was happy, which meant goodwill (or good karma) down the road. Often, if a book was involved, my name showed up in the acknowledgements. Fair enough!

When's the best time of day to write? How many pages (or words) should you turn out each day? How many hours should you schedule for writing, and how many for research? Where should you write—at home, in a special room? Or do you need an office?

Before all else: Understand that when and how much you can write may be affected by the people around you, your immediate family. If you have a spouse or partner, and/or children, your schedule has to take into account their schedules. It's important to plan around others to some extent, if only to avoid interruptions as well as to keep everyone happy.

When to Write?

Writers write at all hours of the day and night. Some prefer the idea of always writing during specific, regular hours, and some don't. I know full-time writers who keep the same hours as they did when they had a job with a steady paycheck. Others, like me, write on a schedule that roughly follows their sleeping habits, adjusted by the dictates of deadlines, family and social demands, the needs of Sophie of Dog, home repairs—and at times even by pure enthusiasm.

The best answer to the question "When should I write?" is "Write when you can."

That sounds flippant, but it's valid. As a part-time writer, you may have found time to write only from after dinner until 9:00 p.m. Or, as Joe Haldeman did (Joe is the award-winning author of *Forever War* and other works) when he was earning his MFA at the Iowa Writers' Workshop, you might get up at 4:00 a.m. and write until it was time to go to work or classes. Joe managed to get in at least 15 hours of writing each week.

Science-fiction writer Mike Resnick stays up late and spends most of the night writing. I kept that schedule, too, for a couple of years, but eventually found going to bed at 5:00 a.m. just too depressing.

Remember: Writing requires not only time, but inclination or willingness. So, plan to write when you have both the time and the necessary mental outlook.

When I Work

I'm very enthused about this book, so when I have a full day available I write from around 9:00 in the morning until early afternoon. Then I knock off for an hour or more for lunch and errands around town. I pick up again at 2:00 p.m. and work straight through until dinner.

After that, I relax for an hour (or three), hit it again until 11:30 p.m., then start to wind down. I've done much the same for past projects, whenever facing on a book deadline. (And yes, I would have resented working such hours for anyone else.)

My normal writing schedule is more typically a tad more relaxed: a couple of hours late in the morning, a couple of hours late in the afternoon, and three or more hours late in the evening. I also set aside an odd hour or two a couple days of the week for related tasks: talking or corresponding with editors, sending invoices, depositing checks, and doing research. Occasionally, research takes up a day or more per week, as was the case with the book I wrote right before this one.

Most of the topics I write about, however, don't require much additional research, as I try to write about things that interest me. I find that I accumulate most of the knowledge I need under the guise of pursuing personal hobbies or engaging in leisure activities like reading.

So that's my schedule six days out of the week, sometimes seven.

I go off this schedule when I'm on vacation (and at tax time). On sunny spring and summer afternoons, I spend extra time working in my yard. I also get out a few evenings or a Saturday now and then by giving lectures or teaching a writing class. All of these breaks are vital; if I didn't get out, I would get stale pretty fast.

When deadlines and finances permit, I take a week (or two or three) for a longer break—sometimes a trip, otherwise just staying at home to relax and catch up on other things. This is not something I do every year. But in a good year, I do it two or three times. After all, this is one of the most appealing aspects of making my own schedule.

Where to Write

When I lead a writer's workshop or speak to a class, this question always arises: "Where is the best place to write?"

Most freelancers write at home, so "at home" is the easy answer. But home is different for every writer. Some live alone, some have roommate(s), a partner, or a spouse. Some have children, and maybe dogs and cats.

Whatever the living situation, all writers need these elements:

- A private room or corner of a room where they can keep the accoutrements of the trade (books, computer, notebooks, etc.)

- A work surface, big enough for a typewriter, computer, or laptop.

- A physical way to prevent disturbance for several hours—like a door to close, a way to ban small children, and enough distance from any distracting activities and noise.

Everything else is personal preference. Music? Sure—I like it (Van Morrison is on the CD player just now), but that's not true for all writers. Allen Wold, for example, who did a number of TV novelizations in the 1980s, said he needed absolute silence to write. (I don't know what he did when his new baby came along.)

Do you need a word processor? Wold wrote all of his novels on legal pads. When finished, he typed the manuscript into his word processor, editing as he went. A nice two-draft system, but it wouldn't work for me. I can't write quickly enough with pencil or pen to keep up with my thoughts. Still, I often do rough outlines by

Saints preserve us!

[D]on't, please, get precious about your working methods. There seems to be some sort of pipsqueak tenet on the matter. Writers presumably have to work from one to three a.m. in a room upholstered in red plush, on purple paper, with an old quill that belonged to their Revolutionary ancestor. Half-baked colleagues of mine are constantly touching off little autobiographical notes such as "I do my Hohokus stories on windy afternoons in the cupola of a haunted barn, writing in Chinese characters with an airbrush."

Saints preserve us! . . .

The more you humor your inadequacies by compensating with phony environment, the tougher your work will become. You have to be in a mood. I grant that. But if you haven't the understanding of yourself to get into any mood when you wish—then don't fool around with the mood business. Be an automobile salesman.

I would like you to be able to write as well as you can with pen, pencil, and typewriter, in tree houses, boiler factories, and on subway trains. I insist that you must be able to write with a stomach-ache, a crying baby, a paving drill going—and on a typewriter that has a non-functioning "e" and an inoperable back-spacer. If you want to and need to.

Then—for your regular surroundings—any moderately quiet, well-ventilated room with an ordinary typewriter table and chair will be paradisical.

You might as well begin correctly in the matter of time, too. Work right after breakfast. Why not?

—Philip Wylie, co-author of the classic novel When Worlds Collide, from an article in The Writer, July 1938 hand, and I also write poetry that way. Otherwise, I usually save my best cursive talents for very important letters—and endorsing those big checks.

Writing is an occupation that doesn't require you to buy a lot of equipment. You don't need a lot of fancy equipment or tools. All you really need is a means of putting words on paper in standard manuscript format. A typewriter still works for many writers.

Some writers get caught up and lost in the trappings of writing. They agonize over which computer or word processor to use, what sort of paper to buy, whether to have printed envelopes for submissions, whether to dictate notes, compose first drafts by hand or at the keyboard, and so on.

If you find yourself fretting about such things, remember that you are not being paid for your tools. You are paid for what you produce with them. Concentrate on what you can do with your tools, not on the tools themselves.

What about an office outside the home? Well . . . that seems a bit presumptuous to me. There are some writers who need to be anywhere but home when they write. Some like to hang out at coffee shops as a place to write—and to observe people on the sly. But a real office in another location seems a needless expense, and perhaps an affectation.

On the other hand, going to the mountains or the beach for a week or three to finish a book seems to me a very practical thing for a writer to do!

What to Write?

Most of us do better work with less effort when we write about something we know.

For part-time writers, I've always advised that they write on whatever they wish—especially when first starting out. But as a full-time writer, you won't always be so free. The necessity of earning a decent living usually precludes it. By writing on subjects you are familiar with, you're less likely to need lots of new research each time. You build up a body of knowledge over time—and important connections with editors interested in those subjects, and experts you can interview for quotes to spice up your articles.

Still, from time to time, try to find a few moments to write something that's more interesting or fun for you personally. At the moment, I have a pair of pet projects going: one is a mystery novel, the other a book about growing up in the 1960s.

These may never be published, but they're fun. And they serve more than one purpose. When I'm stuck on something else, I can turn to one of my pet projects and avoid a case of "writer's block." And I use the books as motivators; working for a few hours on one is a reward I give myself after finishing a tough assignment.

And there's always the chance that these books will see publication some day.

But you need to avoid the temptation to do these pet projects before you've completed that pressing deadline, and sealed the envelope or sent the computer file over the Internet. Let's face it, sometimes the lure of an alternative project—any alternative—is a siren's song leading you off course and into danger— of missing a deadline.

I've often experienced cases like this: I'm writing a short story, due next week for an original anthology. The writing isn't going well. I gripe about how much easier it would be to be writing something more fun, like a celebrity interview. But I don't have any such assignment; I just buckle down and finish the short story.

Ten months later, I am agonizing over that celebrity interview. I have to boil down two hours of a taped interview into a 2,000-word article. Now I remember how "easy" it was to write that short story for that last anthology. But I plow on and finish the interview.

This scenario is fairly common. When I'm about 70 percent

through a nonfiction book, I think it must be easier to write a novel. When I'm writing a novel, I find myself wishing I were writing a nonfiction book—knowing how much "easier" it would be . . .

The subconscious or conscious mechanism at work here is easy to see through. Don't be fooled. When the going gets tough, the tough get writing—ignoring that urge to take a path with apparently less resistance.

The disciplined (and successful) writer puts aside the temptation and finishes the project at hand first. As a full-time writer, you should write that which pays money.

Charity Work?

People will ask you to write for nothing. Such requests come in every now and then. Someone is looking around for someone like you to write for a newsletter or brochure. Someone has a friend who knows this guy over on the west side of town whose partner knows a woman whose friend is a writer. It turns out that's you. Would you mind?

I don't mind charity work—literal or figurative. I've written brochures and put together newsletters and flyers for local Red Cross chapters, museums, political candidates, and so forth. What I do mind is anything that might interrupt and/or delay a paying project or anything I've already committed to doing.

Remember, writing for free without credit given, and/or without publication in a respectable venue, is no way to advance your career. Writing your own novel, short story, article, or nonfiction book adds to your professional credentials and more often will lead to other opportunities for paying work.

Similarly, I turn down most requests to "help" someone with their novel, life story, or whatever. Such offers—usually along the lines of, "I've got a great idea for a book! You write it, and we'll split the money!"—seldom pay, and present many problems.

Even if someone does offer to pay you to critique, edit, or

otherwise help, it probably won't be enough. These projects will eat up lots more time than you think.

Rather than trying to fix someone else's manuscript, why not work on your own? Revise that unsold short story. Get an outline for that book idea down on paper. Any such project has far more potential for you, and fewer entanglements, than working on someone else's writing.

By helping someone with their personal writing project, you risk exposing yourself to their ire if their pet project doesn't turn out as they hoped. Do you want to put yourself in that position? Think twice before you say yes.

This doesn't mean I don't help other writers—or non-writers. I'm just picky about it. There are half a dozen or so books in print today that wouldn't be, if I hadn't become involved with the project. Each was a book that I felt needed to be published, by a writer I felt ought to be published. The same is true for a large number of magazine articles.

I made no money from these. But I felt the writers deserved to be in print. I also knew each of them to be the sort of person who could take advice and criticism, and who would not give up.

I know I benefited from help from other writers early in my full-time career. Those writers who helped me did so in the spirit of "paying forward" rather than paying back the help they received earlier in their career from established writers.

There is really no way to pay back such favors. So, it's paid forward, to help someone else. (If this book helps you, I'll be glad to know it. But I hope you will pay it forward by sharing what you've learned with someone else in turn.)

Just pick your projects carefully. There's only so much of you

---

"You Can't Lose!"

Every town has its characters. The small town where I live—Oxford, Ohio—is populated with dozens of them. One of the more notable characters was a late acquaintance who went by the nickname of "Bang."

Having owned several businesses during his life, and being something of a raconteur, Bang was sure that his life-story needed telling.

So he came to me and offered what he figured was a wager I couldn't refuse: "Write my life-story . . . and if doesn't make a million dollars, I'll pay you ten thousand dollars."

I managed to keep from laughing as I pled being too busy. I did wonder, however, how long I would have to wait for the book to make a million—before he would have to pay me ten thousand dollars.

As it turned out, it was a moot point. He passed away a couple of months later.

to go around. And remember, if you have too much free time: Are you keeping up with sending out queries, or researching markets, or doing record-keeping? Don't neglect taking care of your own business first.

Goals and Measures of Progress

If you're a goal-oriented person, you will set achievable targets for how much time to spend writing each day or week. And you'll know how much writing you should strive to produce in that time.

Goals are a bit like project management tools; they create an implicit schedule. They measure your production and progress, and offer valuable feedback.

What sorts of goals can or should a writer set?

There are many approaches to goal-setting among writers. Some writers measure their work in number of completed pages. For instance, you might plan to turn out five complete pages of your novel per day. By working five days per week, you should produce 25 pages per week. Allowing for interruptions and editing, you can finish 350 pages of a completed manuscript— enough for a typical novel—in less than four months.

This is exactly how many novelists work. Whether it takes 20 minutes or 12 hours, these writers work their way to that goal of five pages per day.

For some, a set number of words is the best goal. If you set a goal of 500 words per day (two or three pages in regular manuscript format), you can write a short story in five days. Or a book chapter in two weeks.

Some of you may prefer to set and measure your goals by a clock. You would prefer to set a minimum number of hours to put in per day or per week. To increase your output, put in more time. But beware: Don't try to measure the quality of your work or value of your time by how long it took you to complete a project. Time is very slippery, and how much work you can do in a given day or hour is affected by many other things—your mood, the project itself, and outside factors.

Freelance writing rarely pays by the hour. Most writing pays by the word, by the project, or sometimes by the page.

Imagine that you have an assignment from a magazine called *Snarling Cat*. An upscale journal for owners of exotic pets, it pays $1.25 per word. Your article of 1,500 words will yield $1,875.

Having completed that, you then get an assignment from *Grinning Dog Magazine* (a publication for owners of pets like Sophie the Dog). For 2,500 words, you get $600. That's 24 cents per word, less than 20 percent of what *Snarling Cat* paid.

There is a good chance you spent about the same time on each article. Or maybe you even put in more time on the article that paid less. But, for the sake of example, let's say you put in about 10 hours on each. Thus, you earned $187.50 per hour on the *Snarling Cat* article, while your time on the *Grinning Dog* article returned less than one-third of that, $60 per hour.

Still, for less than a week of work, your total earnings were decent. And you probably didn't have the choice to do two articles for the higher-paying magazine. So you diversified, and produced two articles, and spent your time well.

Time is a good management tool, but a poor measure of the quality or quantity of your output.

That pretty much covers the basics of managing your work as a writer. As you can see, how, when, and where you work is whatever suits you best. But you need to be honest and realistic, and learn to accept the discipline of whatever course you lay out for

Goals

Goals are easier to reach when they're realistic.

For instance, as I write this, it is late in the evening, and I have added 2,500 words to this chapter today.

So, I tell myself I'm going to see whether I can make it to 3,000 words before I knock off and go to bed.

I'm confident I'll reach the goal—but it's just enough to make me stretch a little.

That's what makes a goal a good one.

It encourages and helps you reach a little farther—to something you sense is achievable.

yourself. Remember: You've chosen this career for its overall flexibility and other rewards. To gain them, you need to buckle down and learn how to make it work for you.

In the next chapter, we'll look at how to manage your work on a deeper level. We'll deal with more abstract issues such as getting yourself to write, learning to handle rejection, and knowing how best to face and solve other potential problems the full-time writer must face.

CHAPTER 4

Getting Yourself to Write

I T IS IMPORTANT THAT YOU WRITE on a regular basis. Indeed, if you don't write frequently, you may find it more and more difficult to the point where you are unable to write.

Writing regularly keeps your mind working in its best "writer's mode." It makes it easier for you to switch to that "writing mind" the next time you sit down to write.

If you write on an irregular schedule, or easily put off writing in favor of something else, you may find that returning to writing is a bit difficult. It's not unlike playing a musical instrument, exercising, juggling, or speaking a foreign language. The longer you stay out of practice, the more difficult it is to get back into it. (You don't necessarily lose your writing skills; rather, it's a matter of getting back into the routine, and tapping your talents, so they become fluent again.)

As a full-time writer, you cannot afford to lose your edge by staying away from your work too long. The reasons are clear:

- Your income (and all that implies) depends on your ability to write.

- The goodwill of editors (perhaps future assignments) depends on your ability to write.

- An extended period away from writing about your core topics can set you back. You get out of the loop, and when you return, much has changed—who's editing and writing what, what topics are hot, and more.

- Your writing capabilities depend on your ability to write. ("Use it or lose it!" can apply to writing, as much as to any other skill.)

Any number of things can stop you from writing or greatly reduce your output. They range from interruptions by presumptuous friends and neighbors to professional setbacks such as unexplained rejection and "writer's block."

The main thing is to find ways to keep writing.

Find Time to Write

When I teach a class for would-be writers, they always have a predictable set of excuses for not writing. The most frequent is a job, followed by household chores and taking care of children.

My first impulse is to ask them why they signed up for the course, but I refrain. Instead, I take a positive approach. I tell them about how I wrote when I was juggling a full-time and a part-time job. Or how I found time to write when I was a scout leader, balancing that with a full-time job and family duties.

The point: you can always find time to write. If you really want to. You may have to sacrifice television or reading time, or skip going out once in a while. But nothing comes without sacrifice—especially something that requires as much time and concentration as writing.

And when you're not actually sitting down to write at a keyboard, you can plan and develop ideas just about anywhere, any time—while driving, while you're walking or doing exercises, as you do household chores or the more automatic parts of your job. You can even work out problems while taking a shower. (I get some of my best ideas there.)

Take notes as you go, with pen and paper, or a tape recorder. Use whatever works for you. Just don't waste any of that valuable time when your body is occupied but your mind isn't.

Get Interruptions Under Control

One of the worst things you can do to a writer is to steal his or her time. That is exactly what problems, distractions, and other sorts of interruptions do.

But that's not the end of it. Any interruption has consequences beyond the immediate loss of time. Whenever you are interrupted, you have to work to recover your focus and return to what you were doing.

Imagine yourself painting the side of a house. You've done all the preparation—you have your ladder and brushes in hand. You mix the paint, set the ladder, and climb up about eight feet.

You dip the brush in the paint, and—oops!—the neighbor's horse comes running into your yard through an open gate, and knocks down the ladder. Down you go, along with the paint, ladder, and brushes!

What do you do? First, you deal with the interruption itself by chasing the horse out of your yard, and close the gate to discourage additional intrusions. Then you have to go through all the preparations again before you can climb the ladder and go back to work.

An interruption to your writing is like being knocked off that ladder. Once you've dealt with the interruption, you then must go through some preparations to get yourself mentally back into your writing.

Set a Routine Time

It is helpful to write always at the same time of day. . . . And it is important that you write something, regardless of quantity, every day.

As the Romans put it, Nulla dies sine linea—No day without a line.

(They were speaking of lines drawn by artists, but the rule applies as well to the writer.)

—B. F. Skinner (quoted in Advice to Writers, edited by Jon Winokur)

Unavoidable Distractions & How to Deal with Them

At times, you have to face larger distractions or interruptions that you cannot ignore. Problems such as an accident or illness (your own or someone else's) come to everyone sooner or later. Serious life changes and catastrophes—and even positive events—can pop up unexpectedly; they will eat seriously into your writing time.

Often, there is no way to get any work done until the problem or situation is resolved. However, when you're up against a deadline, you have a valid need to write. Remember: Your urgent need to continue writing is legitimate.

On the other hand, the urge to write can distract you from dealing with an interruption on a timely basis. Then the distraction slows down your writing, and you end up with a nasty pair of self-reinforcing problems.

My own approach to such quandaries is to take the path of least resistance. I consider which situation I can take care of quickly. Almost without exception, that is the problem that caused the interruption. I deal with the problem and then go back to work. The less I agonize over which to do, the better.

My best advice is to deal with the problem at hand. Do what you must do, or delegate it to someone who can handle it for you. Deal with the intrusive problem, person, or situation first. Hopefully, you've made some allowances in your financial plans—and in scheduling your work—for a small number of interruptions.

An Ounce of Prevention

You've heard, I'm sure, that an ounce of prevention is worth a pound of cure. It's true—which is why we have vaccines, dental checkups, and driver training.

Apply that homily to your writing. Do everything you can to prevent interruptive problems in advance.

How? Whenever you can, schedule any known family matters, chores, social or business engagements, and other commitments in advance, to avoid your peak writing times. You will probably have to plan ahead for at least two weeks.

That leaves you on your schedule with certain hours and days when you know you can work uninterrupted. When those moments arrive, write! You will feel motivated, knowing your other obligations are covered—and knowing the time you have is for writing only.

I know it sounds Zen-like: "Schedule your interruptions around your writing, and schedule your writing around your interruptions." But "schedule" is the key word here; make one, make sure it allows for occasional breaks and interruptions, and then try like crazy to stick to it.

If you don't already, learn to delegate tasks to others. To free up your time for writing, perhaps a spouse or partner can take care of important household and/or family chores. Yes, they are busy, too. But it helps to talk about things long enough in advance (again, the schedule) so that your need for help isn't a surprise. Often, people may complain about helping you because you didn't do them the courtesy of asking long enough in advance; it appears to them that there is no real choice and that you're just taking them for granted. Talking it through will help sort out the real priorities. Especially when you're up

"Mike's Not Working—Get Him to Do It!"

Since you're home and "not doing anything," relatives or neighbors may figure they can get you to help them garden, run errands, or give you a ride somewhere.

This may start the very first day you begin working at home. Most people who call or visit with such requests just forget that you are working. Others can't get the idea in their heads that you can be both at home and yet "at work."

I've learned the hard way to say "no" to most requests. It's tough. Some people will whine and beg—whatever they can think of. But I noticed that every time I took time away from my work to help, it often just encouraged that person to impose on me again.

I finally adopted a policy of always being on deadline—even if it was invented on the spot. "I'm really sorry, but I have to finish what I'm doing before five o'clock, so I can FedEx it to my editor." Sometimes, I'd suggest someone else who might help them, or a different way they could do what they needed to do.

But I made it clear I was working, and that I was under a lot of time pressure. And I was truly sorry that I didn't have the time available to assist. (Which was the truth.)

Soon, people stopped calling for help, and no one was too angry with me. They had grown to understand I was always working hard at my writing business.

And I was.

against a pressing deadline, you may need help taking care of other matters. Just be sure you are prepared to pull your weight at other times, to return the favor and show your gratitude.

Writing on the Road

As a writer, you can take your work with you. On a vacation, family visit, or business trip, you will find that there are quite a few hours that can be used for productive writing.

I've been carrying my work around with me for the past 15 years, and always get some writing done. In 1986 I bought my first laptop (a TRS-80 Model 100 "slab" computer) when I was asked to conduct two seminars at the University of South Florida's annual writer's conference, which ran for five days.

At the time, I was up against two deadlines. But even though my conference time was heavily booked, I wrote whenever there was a spare hour. And I made the deadlines.

I've worked on my writing during family vacations, and on trips like parents' day at my daughter's college. Most of the time, the work gets done sitting in a motel room. Instead of watching TV or reading, I write something. I don't always use a laptop; pen and paper still function as a decent "word processor," if you're not in a big hurry.

Cleaning the Refrigerator?

You can be your own worst source of interruptions. How do I know? Because it's endemic to working alone. Sometimes, you aren't aware of self-interruptions. But you need to watch for this—because you can waste more of your own writing time than can any neighbors, annoying relatives, campaigning politicians, salespeople, or friends in dire need of someone to listen to their latest problems.

Ernest Hemingway called it "cleaning the refrigerator." At times, he liked to write standing up, using the refrigerator as a writing surface. But often, he was distracted by how dirty the refrigerator was, and so ended up cleaning the thing before writing.

But the refrigerator wasn't really that dirty. It was his way of putting off writing.

We all have a refrigerator to clean. Mine is my entire office. As I write these words, I am itching to go through everything, throw out a lot of useless paper, and maybe rearrange bookshelves, lamps, and whatnot. But I'm aware that the cleanup could waste a full day and evening. And three days later, entropy will have put things right back where they were anyway.

Meanwhile, my writing would languish. It would take a bit of effort to get myself back to the writing mode. I'd have to climb back up the metaphorical ladder, after cleaning the metaphorical refrigerator. Sounds exhausting, doesn't it?

Why do we do this to ourselves? I'm convinced that most self-interruption results from one or more of the following:

- "Stage fright"—a fear of not being able to do what you have committed to do, at least not well enough.

- Fear of rejection. We want to be liked for ourselves and for our writing.

- Getting stuck because you can't find just the right way to finish a scene, write an article lead, plot that ending to your novel, rewrite a book chapter, or find a good rhyme.

- Not knowing what you will write.

- Boredom with the writing project at hand.

- Distracting problems—or even anticipation of something positive. Sometimes you won't be aware of the distraction, but it's there.

- Letting yourself get too tired, or falling sick.

Since your writing is, presumably, among the most important things in your life, you want to eliminate all the self-distraction you can. Awareness of its many sources can help give you a handle on the problem. Watch yourself for interruptions. Whenever you stop writing because you just remembered something that had to get done—or someone you had to call, or any of hundreds of other excuses for not writing—stop and ask yourself, "Is this really something I have to do now?"

Then ask yourself what's bothering you about the project you're on. Chances are, answering this more important question will be the real solution. If it's not illness or a bona fide outside interruption, you are likely making up something that must be done because you have a problem with what you are writing.

Or you may have (cue the scream and scary music): Writer's Block!

Writer's Block

Writer's block is a common malady. Most people (especially those who don't write) don't understand it. And many writers don't understand it, either.

If you understand how and why something works, you are halfway to solving your problem. So I propose now to remove the mystery surrounding writer's block.

Ready?

Writer's block is not being able to write. That's it, plain and simple.

Well, okay—there's more to it than that. But writer's block is neither exotic nor mysterious. It's often nothing more than a technical impasse that occurs when you reach a point where you know something is wrong, but can't identify it. The subconscious wants to resolve the problem, and won't let you progress until you do.

When this happens, you can work your way around (or through) the block by writing.

But how can you write if you're blocked? There are two approaches. One is indirect, the other direct. Either will remove whatever roadblocks writer's block has thrown in front of you.

Sneaking Up on Writer's Block

The indirect approach to ending writer's block: Start another writing project. Tackle something you already know will get you going again. This foils your frustration over not accomplishing anything, and gives you the break you need.

After you've been away from the original blocked project for a few days, you'll gain a fresh viewpoint on it. The main thing to remember: Keep yourself away from whatever has you stuck for a few days. That includes even thinking about the problem. So pull out another project to work on and think about.

If you can, give your subconscious up to two weeks. This is more than enough time away from a project. Now your fresh viewpoint will often point right at the hidden problem. And by identifying the problem, you probably now know how to solve it.

Write Through It!

If you have a deadline and must get the work out, you can still write your way out of the block: Write the parts you know how to write first.

Jump ahead in your short story or novel and write a scene you know will take place. You might even write the ending. If you're writing nonfiction, write a book chapter or article section that you already know how to handle.

No help? Outline it! Outline as much as you know, including what you've already written. Then, fill in the blanks between the outline headings.

Eventually you gain a viewpoint or an insight that will help you work out your problem. At the same time, you'll avoid compounding your problems, extending the "block" with frustration.

Just Keep Going

You probably don't write any better when you write slowly than when you write quickly, so make it speedy.
. . .
  Some mornings when I read what I wrote the previous day I think it's fairly entertaining; other times I think it's pure rubbish.
  The main thing is not to take any notice, not to get elated or upset, just keep going.
  —Maeve Binchy, from "Welcome to My Study," in The Writer, February 2000

I can't tell you which approach to take, but when you feel like you have writer's block, try one approach or another. In the rare instance when you have a more serious case of it, admit that you need a brief vacation from writing of any type. You'll come back refreshed and eager to write.

Dealing with Rejection

The prospect of rejection shakes many beginning writers to the core. They worry and procrastinate. Some subconsciously put off writing to avoid rejection. Others seek perfection, and never finish or send out their work.

Unfortunately, rejection is a fact of life for writers. There's no avoiding it; even after more than 25 years of writing, I get rejected. All the polishing and perfection in the world can't prevent it.

There are many ways to reduce the possibility of rejection, but there is no way to guarantee you won't be rejected.

So, stop worrying about rejection. I won't suggest that you should "embrace" rejection, but you should get used to it. You'll probably never become completely immune to rejection, but you can reduce its negative effects.

Living with Rejection

The best way to reduce the pain of rejection is to get used to it. Which means submitting a lot of manuscripts and queries. Get enough rejections, and you'll gradually be desensitized.

Another trick is to keep several queries and submissions in circulation most of the time. This tends to reduce the effect of any one rejection. If you have three manuscripts and queries circulating, a rejection is going to hurt only one-third as much as if you had only one submission out.

Remember: Rejections are not personal. Editors who bounce a submission don't do so because you're too young or too old, live in a bad part of town, are missing some teeth, or for any reason having to do with you personally. Editors don't know your age, religion, race, or anything else about you, beyond your name and the kind of writing you do (and any information you might have shared with them willingly). It is your work that is accepted or rejected—not you.

Perhaps to your amazement, you'll be happy to know that rejections aren't even always based on the quality of your work. Editors reject good manuscripts all the time, for many reasons that have nothing to do with quality. Here are just a few:

- The magazine or book publisher is overstocked.

- Your manuscript is good but too long, or too short.

- The editor bought something similar last week.

- The editor has a personal prejudice against your topic.

- The editor is having a bad day.

- The old editor quit or was fired, and the new editor isn't buying.

- The publisher is going out of business.

- The editor is a mindless barbarian with the literary taste of a bag of rocks.

No matter the reason for a rejection, it is beyond your control. You can't undo it.

Instead, work on things you can control. You may be able to turn a rejection into something really positive. Submit something else to the editor as quickly as possible following the rejection. At the very least, your name will be familiar. At best, your new submission may avoid whatever caused the first rejection and so impress the editor that he or she accepts it.

Otherwise, start a new project, or rewrite the piece that was rejected—and submit it elsewhere.

All Writers Get Rejection Slips

All writers get rejection slips. Pearl Buck received a rejection for one of her short stories the very week she was notified she had won the Nobel Prize for Literature!

It's part of the writing business: If you aren't getting rejected, you aren't attempting to break into new markets or explore new writing options.

—Dennis E. Hensley, co-author of Write on Target (1995), from an article, "Beating the Odds of Rejection," in The Writer's Handbook 2002

The Case of the Ambiguous Rejection

Not every rejection you get will be useful. I recall the first time I submitted a short story to a science fiction magazine called Amazing Stories.

This was early in my writing career. Not knowing whether I should include a note with the manuscript, I added a brief, half-page missive.

I remember only one line of my note. I closed my little cover letter with the sentence, "Any comments or criticism will be appreciated."

The manuscript was returned a couple of weeks later. There was no rejection slip. There was, in fact, no communication from the editor, save for one word scrawled at the bottom of my own note:

"Sorry"

To this day, I don't know whether the editor was expressing regrets on turning down the story, or commenting on the quality of the story itself.

▲▲▲▲▲▲▲▲▲▲▲▲▲▲▲▲▲▲▲▲▲▲▲▲▲▲▲▲▲▲

Learning from Rejection

All this does not mean you should ignore rejections—far from it! You can learn a lot of good things from rejections.

If an editor includes a note that explains why you were rejected, it means your work impressed him or her enough to elicit a comment. This means you came close. Pay attention to any comments you receive from editors, even the "Nice, but not for us" scrawls. And if you receive any sort of criticism, give it careful consideration. The editor didn't write it to annoy you; he or she wrote it because your work was good enough to make better.

And if an editor asks for a rewrite, by all means do it!

Even with form rejection slips, an editor may add a note—the publisher is overstocked, changing direction, or perhaps no longer buying from freelancers.

Generic rejections also tell you this: If you continue receiving them after three or four submissions, that market's not for you!

Motivational Techniques

Motivation is a reason to put forth effort to accomplish something. Sometimes we understand our motivations. Sometimes we don't.

As a full-time freelancer, one of the most important things you can do is put some thought into what motivates you. And learn to motivate yourself.

Why? Because there will be times when you absolutely, flat-out do not want to write, even though you must. I'm not talking about having to take two days off to travel to a funeral on the other side of the country, or to be in someone's wedding. There are all sorts of extended, slow-motion disasters that can make writing difficult. But if you do not write, you will find yourself in financial or emotional disaster, and eventually you'll just wash out as a full-timer.

You need to learn simple techniques to keep writing, through good times and bad, even in the midst of disaster.

As a full-time writer, you will find that some motivations acquire a new importance. The urgency of deadlines, the growing sense of accomplishment, and the delight in seeing one's efforts succeed are amplified. And money becomes a key issue.

Sometimes these conventional motivations for writers are not enough. They are too ever-present and familiar. Plus, there is the risk that motivations can become distractions; financial needs or the pressure to perform well can turn against you. When this happens, you must turn to more specific tools for self-motivation.

Self-Motivation for Writers

I keep myself writing with a system of ten positive motivators. Try them yourself to boost your productivity. They will see you through hard times, and you can use them daily to eliminate small losses to procrastination. You will write better and enjoy it more.

1. *Ask editors for clear deadlines.* Deadlines spur you to complete projects like nothing else. They instill a feeling of specific value in your work, and enhance the feeling of accomplishment once you've completed the work. If your editor doesn't set a deadline for you, or if you aren't working with an editor, set a deadline for yourself.

2. *Set goals within goals.* Intimidated by a book project (or by the prospect of writing a lengthy article or story)? Don't take on the entire project at once. Break it up into manageable sections. Assign goals of a certain number of words or pages to be completed within a certain time frame. When you reach each goal, assign yourself a new one. This step-by-step method makes a deadline less imposing, and a large project seem smaller. If you try to bull your way through and tackle the whole project all at once by telling yourself, "I *will* finish it," you may find yourself procrastinating—or rushing to complete the job at the expense of quality.

3. ***Set reasonable goals, and adjust them as needed.*** If you wear yourself out producing, say, 3,000 words a day, or if you consistently fall short of your goal, it's time to reassess your ability and the goal. Constant pushing and failure leads to frustration, and you can't do your best work under this kind of pressure. Also, be aware that you may sometimes have to forego meeting a goal for reasons beyond your control.

4. ***Schedule your writing for your best time of day.*** Don't waste your writing time by scheduling it during periods when you know you will be interrupted, and don't rush into writing before you've completed other obligations. Pick the time of day most suited to your creativity, and try to take care of all other obligations before this time.

5. ***Stop writing while you're still "hot."*** Strange as it may seem, it is best to stop work on a project for the day before you get tired of it—provided you've made significant progress. Driving yourself to write until you've exhausted your creativity and enthusiasm can leave you with an empty feeling, and you'll be reluctant to return to your work later. Conserve your

creativity and enthusiasm by stopping while you still have some! You'll be more eager to resume the next day.

6. *Have fun.* Yes, some elements of writing are drudgery. But you can allow yourself a little fun. Intersperse your favorite types of writing projects among your more serious work, to provide a break and to put variety into your writing life. If you write nonfiction, keep a "pet" fiction or poetry project on hand. If you're a fiction writer, begin a nonfiction article or book project.

7. *Keep a daily log of your writing accomplishments.* Find an appointment book with several blank lines for each day of the year. On the pages, log every query, outline, article, story, book, chapter, or portion thereof you complete, each day. Also note telephone calls or trips related to writing. You'll find that you have a desire to do something every day, so you can fill up the blank spaces! Also, previous days' pages give you a clue to your most effective work habits, while providing cumulative evidence that you are accomplishing something.

8. *Reward yourself.* Acceptance letters, checks in payment, and other external rewards aren't always quick to arrive. So give yourself a reward after completing difficult or lengthy projects. Buy a book, take a trip, eat a peanut-butter sandwich, go to a movie—whatever constitutes a reward for you. This reinforces your feeling of accomplishment, and provides additional incentive for your next big project.

9. *Stay busy.* This may seem obvious, but many beginning writers ignore it. Instead of plunging right into the next new article or story after completing a work, an inexperienced writer

may put the manuscript in the mail and do nothing more until it has been accepted or rejected—worrying all the while. This not only wastes time, but also leads to frustration and loss of momentum. Always have a new project in the works. This keeps you in a forward-looking frame of mind, and helps establish a pattern of productivity, the key to writing discipline.

10. *Force yourself to take time off.* We all need a vacation now and then. On occasion, it's okay to give in to the temptation to do something besides write. And don't make your "vacation" too short. If you plan to take a day, take two instead. The first day may recharge you, but the second will build real enthusiasm for writing. By the time you do go back to work, you'll be completely refreshed and eager to produce.

Self-Discipline for Writers

Discipline is slightly different from motivation. Motivation is a driving cause or reason for doing something, but discipline is the basic pattern you establish to keep doing something, even when you forget why or don't believe you can do it.

You must finish a chapter, an article, a story, a rewrite—and in a short period. But what if you can't get into the groove, or can't think of what you're going to write? The irresistible force (distraction) is pitted against the immovable object (deadline).

How do you keep going when the going gets tough? You don't have to be tough—you just have to be willing to work. You need self-discipline.

Writer's write. It's what we do, day in and day out. Successful freelance writers are successful, to a great degree, because they have mastered the basics of discipline.

The Mechanical Approach

Stuck? Don't stop writing. This is when you need the self-discipline to sit down at your desk and keep writing. If inspiration or key information fails you at a given point in your writing, jump ahead in the project and write what you know. Or go back and edit earlier sections of the project.

No help? It's time to fall back on certain mechanical techniques. Pull out and rewrite a portion of something you've already published. Or rewrite a passage by one of your favorite writers.

Still no help? It's time to do mindless mental pushups. Get a published work of your own, or someone else's—it doesn't matter—and start typing the work, copying it word for word. Physically "walk" yourself through the act of writing.

Do this for at least five minutes. At some point, you will find that you've put yourself back in the groove. I can't say exactly how long it will take, but eventually, the stimulus of the sterile writing exercises will steer your mind back to creative writing. (I'm not sure whether this really stimulates me, or just convinces me that I'd rather be doing some creative writing because this copying is so boring. But it works.)

Self-Denial?

Another approach is to cut yourself off from anything you find positive. This is a bit stoic

The Power of Positive Thinking

It's true: Positive reinforcement works better than negative. Too much of life hits us with negative motivations. If you do something (or don't), then a negative thing will happen.

As children, we were quite often handed negative motivation: Get good grades—or you're grounded. Push or hit someone on the playground—and you get punished.

As adults, it is more of the same. Miss your car payments, and you lose your car. It's usually very basic and commonsense.

But why not look at such things in a positive manner? Make your car payments, and keep your car!

Human nature tends to make us turn away from negative motivations, or push against them. But we strive to gain positive rewards.

So whenever you can, turn negatives into positives. Rather than thinking, "If I don't get this book done, I won't have money for a vacation," instead try this: "When I get this book done, I will have the money for a nice vacation!"

for me, but there are writers who claim it works. Deny yourself any entertainment, and any pleasure, until you get unstuck and back to work. No reading, no TV, radio, Internet, etc.

My friend Gene Wolfe works this way. He says it helps push his subconscious into coming up with ideas. Other writers, such as Annie Dillard, banish themselves from their usual surroundings in order to coax the muse.

Others prefer a system of small rewards as interim goals are reached. This may be just the thing you need to get yourself going. Work with the promise to yourself that, as soon as you've completed specific phases of the work, you will do something nice for yourself.

For this to work for me requires the following:

First, I take the reward program seriously, and don't compromise by taking a reward a bit early or if I fall short of my goal.

And second, my favorite reward must involve getting out and away from my workplace. This is the real reward. Working my way through the project then becomes a means of escape, a freedom from the pressure.

Relaxation Techniques

Sometimes you must get away from writing. When switching to another project doesn't help, and you simply cannot motivate yourself, it's time for a break.

Unless you have a really pressing deadline, take a mini-vacation from writing. It can be as long as a week, or as brief as an afternoon and evening.

During this break, do anything but write. Try to avoid thinking about the project that's troubling you. Clean house (yes, even the refrigerator), take a walk, watch TV, read a book, go window shopping, or drive into the next county to treat yourself to a meal or some different scenery. It doesn't really matter what you do— just do something. Get up and get away from your work.

Sometimes you need to do this even if a deadline looms. Take a day, or a few hours—as much as you can spare—and do not write. Do not think about writing, do not worry. Get out! To take a proper break from writing, you must be able to let go. Let go of your writing and your worries.

This is easier said than done. Some people just have too strong a sense that you cannot take time off just when you feel the most pressure to complete a task. But when you reach this point, it may be most vital that you take a break, to catch your breath before you plunge back into completing the work at hand.

Sometimes, it helps to remove yourself from familiar surroundings. I've used this technique often, and often manage to combine writing with the distancing. I go to parks to relax and make notes, or work with my laptop computer. One recent January, I went to Florida, escaping the Ohio winter for three weeks. I spent most of the time there on the back porch of a relative's house, writing a book.

Clear Your Mind

There are any number of approaches to clearing your mind, so you can let go of worries. Yoga, regular exercise, T'ai Chi, or even brisk walking touches the physical and spiritual resources you have within you.

Other relaxation techniques such as meditation and breathing exercises help you keep working when you don't want to, overcome distractions, and otherwise benefit your working life as well as your private life.

One technique I often use is basic visualization. I visualize being in a state where the work is done, the project is completed, or the problem has been solved. There are two steps involved: First, I imagine how good I will feel, after the problem has been solved and the distractions have gone away. Second, once I have that feeling, I hold on to it, and return to it in my mind—that positive feeling—whenever the distraction tries to intrude again or I feel my commitment flagging.

Just Keep Going

John Updike has written more than 50 books by setting a target of writing three pages a day, or roughly 1,000 words a day, six days a week.

His intent is "to do something every day, to advance that particular idea [at hand], and in that way you do accumulate quite a lot of manuscript.

Then he often takes the afternoon off to play golf or engage in other activities.

The results of his steady, consistent writing include the nation's highest literary honors, including two Pulitzer Prizes and the National Book Award.

—from an interview by Leonard Lopate with John Updike in The Writer, July 2001

This basic visualization takes just a few minutes, sometimes in combination with some sort of relaxation exercise, too, like deep, slow breathing.

Give it a try. Any regular practice of modest exercise, mediation, or other "centering" and relaxation technique will help you immensely. It won't solve your problems, but it will give you the energy and desire to focus on what you need to do.

Do These Techniques Work?

My answer: an unequivocal "Yes!" I have used most of these techniques (and know others who have) to keep writing through just about everything. Consider the following.

The only time I was hospitalized in the past 40 years (since childhood), I managed to write three magazine articles—right there in my hospital bed, over an 11-day period. I sold those articles, too. (Ironically, this was the beginning of my move to become a full-time writer.)

Some years back, my spouse was hospitalized for two weeks, but I was still able to write regularly, despite having to work a full-time job, and also care for a five-year-old and a one-year-old.

I've written my way through all sorts of family emergencies, personal problems, and just about any other kind of distraction one might imagine.

I'm not Superwriter. There have been two periods of my life during which I absolutely could not write. The first time was a bad two-year period during which I was divorced, hit by a car, and lost my house. Several important people in my life passed away. It was a rough time. (Some of the things that happened were impossible, too!—such as getting hit by my own car, and later suffering a concussion when I accidentally fell into a marble windowsill in my sleep. Odd misadventures, to be sure, but you get the idea.)

I couldn't write during that time, but it was my great fortune to be able to live on book royalties for those two years.

The second episode occurred not long ago, when I had to deal with another string of misfortunes involving people close to me: dreaded late-night phone calls summoning me to a hospital, a jail, and other unlikely places. At the same time, I was in a desperate financial situation due to the September 11, 2001, attacks that caused work projects for several publishers—more than half of my year's income—to be canceled.

The stress overload was compounded by a pressing health problem. But I did manage to complete this book. How did I do it? Lots of motivation (deadlines!), lots of self-discipline, and lots of relaxation techniques.

I believe I used every technique I just described to you to get this book finished. Yes, they work. And while you may turn to them in times of stress, they work just as well in good times; they will help your writing career move ahead more quickly and with more personal satisfaction. Don't give up these patterns when things start to go well. Make them part of your life-long habits.

As for a full-time freelance writer, there are no acceptable excuses for not writing. Hopefully, you now have some idea of what you can and must do to keep yourself writing.

Now, it's time to take a serious look at yourself, your talents and skills, your accomplishments, and your overall life situation. Are you really ready to make the leap to full-time writing?

Planning and Working Go Hand in Hand

Plan your work . . . then work your plan.

—Norman Vincent Peale

CHAPTER 5

Are You Ready?

BY NOW, YOU MAY BE FIRED UP and ready to give due notice at work. Or maybe you'd just like to walk out, or call in for the last time, perhaps punctuated by a rousing Bronx cheer. But even if "Take This Job and Shove It" is your theme song, you need to give careful thought to this question:

"Are you really ready?"

I don't mean ready to leave your job. An overwhelming desire to go elsewhere—a willingness to quit your day job—has little to do with being prepared to take on a full-time writing career.

To discover if you are ready, you need to evaluate certain things. These include your professional skills, your attitude, experience, your personal living and relationship situations, and other pertinent elements. Helping you do that is the purpose of this chapter.

Let's assume you have been writing part-time, and getting paid well for that work. You have convinced yourself and the real world out there that you are a professional part-time writer, serious about your work. That is a good beginning—but it is but one of six key factors to examine closely before you make the leap into full-time writing.

Measuring Your Readiness: Six Factors

The major factors that can affect (and effect) a writer's success are skills, experience, professionalism, finances, personal life situation, and attitude.

Skills

Certainly, you must have writing ability. But there are related skills that are essential. Do you have solid editing skills? Editing yourself requires a certain honesty that enables you to look at your work and know when there is something wrong with it.

Research skills are important, whether you will write nonfiction or fiction. Do you know where to find what you need to know—or whom to ask?

Do you have solid marketing savvy? Can you research markets for your writing? This is of paramount importance. You'll need to scout out general markets for what you write, and also know how to research specific markets in depth.

Finally, a successful writer has good "people skills." Can you deal with editors, without seeming too pushy or too shy? Can you talk about something other than yourself and your writing? This is more important than you may think. Can you put yourself in an editor's shoes, to understand what he or she needs from you? And it doesn't hurt to be good at the art of flattery. If you know how to compliment an editor for their judgment and editorial skills, without seeming too sycophantic, it just may lead to more work in the future.

Basically, are you a pleasant person to work with? Since editors have lots of writers clamoring to be published, they naturally look for people they can work well with. Is that you?

If you do interviews or other research involving people, you need a certain amount of charm. You don't want to turn off those who have (or have access to) the information you need. You need to be able to draw them out, to convince them to share the kind of information that they have. And you need to write a piece that is fair, honest, and doesn't lead to any lapse of good judgment or basic professional ethics. (A hint: Nearly everyone's second-favorite topic—after themselves—is their work.)

Experience

If you intend to write full-time, you presumably have publishing credits—magazine articles, short stories, novels, and/or nonfiction books. But that is only the beginning.

Your publishing credits must be of a significant number and magnitude. What does that mean? There is no absolute number I can posit that indicates, "Okay—you qualify for a full-time writing career."

After all, anyone who can write at a ninth-grade reading level can amass dozens of publishing credits in little time—by submitting articles, short stories, and poems to small-press journals, fan magazines, and similar periodicals. If you also add in a few opinion pieces or newsy local items for newspapers, and perhaps pen some press releases and newsletter articles for nonprofit organizations, you can show a long list of credits.

But these are non-paying markets. (Those that do pay may just offer $10 or $20 at most.) This is not a foundation for a professional writing career.

Similarly, there are book publishers happy to publish a manuscript, but which pay only modestly for the work required. The academic press fits that description. Academicians who must "publish or perish" provide plenty of fodder for these publishers; they can do plenty of writing in connection with their paid jobs, often helped by sabbatical or research grants. As good as such books are, having published one or two of them does not mean you are likely to succeed in switching to a real writing career.

Start Small and Grow

Big jobs usually go to [those] who prove their ability to outgrow small ones.

—Ralph Waldo Emerson

Before they send you a decent-paying contract, commercial book publishers will expect to see proof of mainstream writing credits, showing that you can write the sorts of books they sell.

Using the same logic, self-publishing credits will not help, unless your sales record from such personally funded endeavors is truly significant and profitable.

All of this points to an important and inescapable fact: You must establish a good part-time writing career before moving to full-time.

By starting part-time, you will have gained experience doing lots of substantial rewrites. Have you been able to revise and sell a piece that was originally rejected? This shows rewrite skills and good market sense.

Have you sold more than one manuscript to the same publisher? A professional needs to be able to do this—to build a relationship with satisfied customers.

And unless you have done very well with writing strictly in one genre of fiction, you will generally benefit from being able to write more than one type of material. Markets in any one field are often limited. To be able to create a full-time career, you may need to consider developing more than one specialty.

A solid range of professional interests will prove to be an important plus in a well-rounded career.

Professionalism

What is professionalism in writing? First, it means that you consistently put your best work forward. That means not compromising; you don't take the easy route with hastily written, poor-quality material. You may find yourself tempted on occasion to do this—perhaps the market allows it, or deadlines threaten. Don't; weak material can come back to haunt you. Who knows what potential client has read that poor example of your work—and assumes that it is the best you can do? You will never hear that they have crossed you off their list of prospects.

On the other hand, good work attracts attention—and leads to more offers that will come to you out of the blue.

Timely delivery of manuscripts—even if the deadline has been rushed ahead in the schedule to serve the publisher's convenience—is essential. Can you say you've done this consistently?

Do you turn in "clean" content? This means no "borrowing" from other sources, and not glossing over crucial subject matter. (The only time you can minimize coverage of an important topic is when you need to cut for length.)

Last, but certainly not least, can you write under any conditions, in any situation? Whether the city decides to jackhammer your street to pieces the day before a deadline, or your computer crashes and you have to retrieve a backup disk, or Sophie the Dog really does chew to pieces your written notes from your last interview—do you know how to carry on and fix the problem without losing too much sleep?

Financial Situation

Financial problems have been the undoing of many a good writer. The first time you come up a bit short, you may ask yourself if this is going to be a repeating situation. Well, it can be—if you let it distract you from your work.

If you allow the situation to become dire, you may have to take a job. And even a part-time job eats enough time that you may soon have to drop from the ranks of the full-time freelancers back to part-time status.

Other pressures will come to bear, depending on your situation. If a family depends on you, you'll feel that pressure even more quickly.

What do you do? The best thing is to plan ahead. Don't let things get to the point where you have to start thinking how you can bring in a lot of money right now. Writing doesn't work that way.

On Persistence

A professional writer is an amateur who didn't quit.

—Richard Bach

Before anything else, do you have a savings account that can function as a serious financial cushion? Do you have a savings account set up for your writing business only—a cash reserve into which you can place funds needed for tax payments, or to spread out early payments for book advances that you'll need to make last until the next check comes in?

You don't want to have to dip into long-term investments or retirement money, just to keep a roof over your head and your writing dream alive.

So a big savings account is important. How big? At least enough to live on for six months. I admit I had saved only enough for two months' living expenses—which turned out to be not enough. Some writers recommend that you save enough to see you through a whole year, or even two. While that may be prudent, it also has the downside of not putting enough pressure on you to work hard from day one of your new commitment to full-time writing. Six months should be enough in my opinion—but just barely.

And don't forget that you need to create an accurate, thorough budget for the actual expenses related to your writing activities. See Chapter 6 for advice on putting that together.

When you switch from part-time to full, you will have more than double the time to write, but that doesn't necessarily mean your income will double—or even if it does, that this will happen in the first two or three months.

Personal Situation

Now we come to something more important than money. Your personal situation—your relationship with your partner or spouse—can erode rapidly if your partner does not support you 100 percent in your decision to write full-time.

This can create a potential distraction, which may prove worse than money problems. If your partner works a day job, and you do not bring in your fair share of income to the household, you can almost count on him or her growing resentful of you for not "going to work." That is courting disaster.

There is only one approach to resolving this kind of conflict. Do everything you can to be certain that your partner is behind you all the way.

Plan ahead.

Establish a healthy cash reserve.

Don't take the leap to writing full-time until you're really ready and have established the solid groundwork to succeed.

And be willing to step outside the writing life to bring in some additional money, if and when it becomes necessary. Even if this may seem a setback to your writing career, this move may preserve your partner's long-term support for your freelance endeavors—knowing that you're willing to put it aside temporarily when this is the most practical thing to do. You can maintain a blind faith in your abilities, but don't expect your partner to feel the same. Be prepared to show her or him the money. And commit to focusing your writing business on doing what it takes to earn it.

Keep this relationship healthy and supportive. Not taking the time or energy to do this may undermine even your best efforts.

Attitude

Maintaining the right attitude is also important. How you feel about yourself can affect your work. At the same time, how you feel about your work affects you.

Inspiration?

A few months after I left my job, I remember telling Andrew Offutt, a writer of my acquaintance, that he was one of the people who inspired me to go into writing full-time. "Good gawd!" he replied. "I hope you won't hold me responsible!"

I suspect Andy was more than half-serious. He knew what I had yet to face along the rocky road of writing.

Similarly, some years later, a writer approached me at a convention to announce that he was going to quit his job and write for a living. And he confessed that I had inspired him to do this.

Flashback! "Um . . . well," I stuttered, "good luck. Do you have anything going?"

"Oh, yes! I have published about twenty articles," he replied, beaming with pride. "Plus, I have a contract for a computer book."

I didn't have the heart to tell him not to quit his day job. But that was my first thought. My second thought: I hope he didn't have a family to support.

As the folk adage goes, "One swallow does not a summer make."

Nor does a single book contract provide enough justification to leave a regular job.

You want to be positive about your work and its potential. If you have a setback, don't treat it like the end of the world. Just continue writing. (You may have to resort to the relaxation techniques in Chapter 4, to release your negative feelings about the setback.)

At the other end of that spectrum, you don't want to be too positive. Pretending (or believing) you are such a good writer that you will never have to worry about income can be unrealistic. I find it helps to imagine myself dead in the water: low on money and with no immediate assignments or prospects. I've learned from hard experience that it's not a bad idea to temper a positive attitude with a dose of skepticism. If you are too positive, you will delude yourself into thinking something will just "come along." Instead, you should be aggressively chasing down work, long in advance.

Several times, I found myself counting on something (a contract, an assignment, a check arriving by a certain date), and it didn't materialize. Besides many tentative deals that "fell through," I've had experiences like a signed contract canceled while I was waiting for the advance check. So I've learned not to count on something until I have it in my hands.

So while you should keep a positive attitude about pending or promised work, be thinking about what you can do instead if the deal falls through.

The Value of Persistence

All the writers I know have one thing in common. (Yes, they all appear to be able to write, but sometimes that's a subjective judgment; just ask any editor who has spent a month editing every sentence of a manuscript to make it publishable.)

The common trait is Persistence (with a capital "P"). Most would-be writers end up quitting because they are not persistent in writing—or in submitting their work. Consider these statistics:

- On average, of the people I meet attending writers' conferences, only one out of twenty actually will succeed in getting published.

- The highest-circulation writers' magazine in the United States has an annual turnover (people who stop subscribing or buying the magazine) of 40 percent. Among the 60 percent retained for the first year, of course, many will drop out the second year.

- A majority (a bit over half) of the people I know who say they want to write have never written a manuscript to completion.

- Of those who have written a complete work, perhaps 10 percent don't ever submit it. And of the 90 percent who do, few will resubmit a manuscript after an initial rejection.

Clearly, writers who become published writers are a minority.

I firmly believe that those who get published do so because they are persistent. (Once into that group, writers who are published again and again become the majority, rather than the minority.)

I know that persistence has saved me more than once during my writing career (both in the part-time and the full-time phases). I've watched some of my best writing get bounced by publisher after publisher—after which I've submitted it again

The Novelist Who Refused to Give Up!

Andrew Offutt, a writer mentioned earlier in this chapter, may be the King of First-Novel Submissions.

Not long after after winning an Atlantic Monthly short story contest while in college, Andy decided to write a novel.

Which he did. He then submitted the manuscript, and resubmitted it, and resubmitted it—over 80 times.

Fortunately, it was published in the end and became the beginning of a nice career as a novelist (under Andy's own name, and various pennames). And that writing career apparently inspired his son, Chris Offutt, whose novels, short stories, and memoirs have gained both popular and critical praise.

In contrast, I felt like someone who hadn't paid his dues when my first book sold to the first editor who saw it.

I didn't feel that way for long. My next two books had to be submitted to three and four publishers before being accepted.

Although Andy's tale of 80-plus submissions is the exception, it does say a lot about the role of persistence.

and again, until it was published. That's how my first two short stories got into print: I submitted each to seven different magazines before they sold to *Isaac Asimov's Science Fiction Magazine* back in 1978.

Curiously, those first two stories have each been reprinted three times since their initial publication.

I have repeated that pattern (albeit with fewer submissions) with several of my books.

In my opinion, persistence as a trait remains one of the strongest indicators of a writer's real chance of professional success.

A Self-Scoring Readiness Test

When I first outlined this book, I made a note for this section that said, "Four points for honesty." I did that to remind myself to tell you that honesty counts for a lot in the writing business.

I mean being honest with yourself. Are you? Can you admit to yourself the times in your life, for instance, when you've done things for petty or stupid reasons, without blaming someone else?

If you can be that honest with yourself, then I figure you can honestly assess your readiness to go into a full-time writing career, in the questionnaire that follows. Which puts you ahead of many people.

No infallible test exists to tell whether you are suited to write for a living. Still, I have an idea of some of the fundamental qualities necessary to succeed in this wacky business, and this easy test will help you pinpoint just how ready you are.

That is, if you are honest.

Please reply "Yes" or "No" to the questions in each of the six categories that follow. You will find a guide to scoring your answers at the end of this chapter.

Skills

1. Are you a good typist?_____

2. Are you good at one-on-one communication? _____

3. Can you rely on your editing skills to fix what's wrong with a manuscript? _____

4. Do you consistently use a spell-check program? _____

5. Do you know where to find information, or whom to ask, when you need to research a subject that is outside your experience? _____

6. Are you good at searching out information on the Internet? _____

7. Can you use a public library? _____

8. Do you know different approaches to analyzing a market? _____

9. Have you had consistent success based on your market analyses? _____

Experience

10. Have you published a book? _____

11. Have you published more than one book? _____

12. A short story or magazine article? _____

13. More than 20 articles? _____

14. Are two or more of your works with the same publisher? _____

15. Have you ever resubmitted a rejected manuscript to another publisher? _____

16. Have you rewritten and improved a rejected manuscript, without being asked? _____

17. Are there manuscripts tucked away in a closet or desk that you have "retired," because you realized they were not publishable in their current form? _____

18. Has any of your work been reprinted or excerpted? _____

19. Have you written a second edition of any of your books? _____

20. Ever had an editor contact you with a book idea, and ask if you would like to write that book? _____

21. Have you faced and overcome an episode of "writer's block?" _____

22. Have you published in more than one subject area (in more than one genre, if your work is fiction)? _____

Professionalism

23. Do you take rejections in stride? _____

24. Have you learned anything positive from rejections? _____

25. If you have had a bad review, did you learn something from it? _____

26. Do you put forth the same amount of effort and attention

into low-paying assignments as you do for high-paying assignments? _____

27. Are you scrupulous about deadlines? _____

28. Do you work to assure that you aren't glossing over information that could be vital to your topic? _____

29. Have you ever voluntarily done a major rewrite of some or all of your work on an assignment, before submitting it, because you knew it wasn't your best writing? _____

Financial Situation

30. Do you have a savings account? _____

31. Would you be able to live on your savings for six months?

32. Do you always pay your bills on time? _____

33. Do you have three or fewer credit cards? _____

34. Do you have a good relationship with a bank? _____

35. Has your writing income as a part-time writer equaled at least half of your job income for more than a year? _____

36. Do you have a credit reserve? _____

37. Are you married or with a partner? _____

38. Can you reduce your monthly expenses? _____

Personal Situation

39. Is your partner in agreement with you about your plans to write full-time? _____

40. Is your partner agreeable to supporting you for up to a year, while you ramp up your writing career? _____

41. If a financial crisis hit, would you be willing to take on a part-time or full-time job? _____

42. Are you assured of having a minimum of six hours per day available to work on your writing, five days each week? _____

43. Can you go without socializing for a week or more, when you need to finish a project? (No going out with friends, no telephone or Internet chats, etc.) _____

Attitude

44. Do you handle criticism well? _____

45. If requested changes do not alter meaning, are you willing to make changes in your work in order to sell, even if you disagree with how necessary or helpful they are? _____

46. Are you really persistent, without being a pest? _____

47. Can you recognize when a project is not worth continuing? _____

48. If someone breaks a promise, can you accept it, and move along to something else? _____

49. Do you feel that you are competing with other writers? _____

Score the Test

Let's take a look at your test results. Remember: Your score is an indicator of whether you have traits that favor success. It is not an absolute prediction of success or failure, since there are many unpredictable forces at work in a writing career—often from sources outside of your control.

To score this test, give yourself five (5) points for each "Yes" answer. Then compare your total to the following key:

100-110 points: You have a good shot at being successful.

80–95 points: You should build up a few more publishing credits—and your savings account—before jumping into full-time writing.

60–75 points: Think about it for another year, and keep writing!

40–55 points: Don't quit your day job yet.

0–35 points: Full-time writing is probably not your thing.

This simple test may help you identify some weaknesses. If you score low, but still wish to move ahead toward your dream of becoming a full-time freelance writer, go back to your lowest scoring answers and review them carefully. Ask yourself: What can I do—what would be the best way over the next three months, six months, and one year—to improve that part of my readiness?

If and when you are satisfied that you are ready to make the leap to full-time writing, it's time to make preparations. Chapters 6 and 7 will help you with that.

CHAPTER 6

Financial Planning for Writers

A S A PART-TIME WRITER, you may have viewed your writing income as a way to bring in extra money, a way to pay for special things you couldn't otherwise afford. If your part-time writing income took a dip, you didn't have to worry about losing your house or car, having enough to eat or to pay utility bills, having your spouse angry at you, and so on.

But if your full-time writing income takes a plunge, it can be a disaster. Can your spouse or partner support you and the rest of the household on his or her income? If not, you'll have to dig deeply into savings or borrow money to pay bills.

You want to write for reasons besides keeping the money rolling in. Still, financial planning is central to a full-time writing career, just as for any self-employed person.

Changes in Your Household Budget

Before you make the leap to become a fully self-employed writer, you need to review your current monthly living expenses. When you total everything on which you spend money, your current budget may look something like this ($2,489 per month, or $29,868 per year):

Figure 6-1. Monthly Budget (before freelancing)

Category *Subcategory*		*Totals*
Housing		
Rent or House Payment	*759.26*	
Incidental and Improvements	*90.00*	
		849.26
Telephone		35.00
Utilities		
Gas & Electric	*225.00*	
Water	*72.00*	
		297.00
Car Payments		323.84
Car Expense		
Gasoline	*80.00*	
Parking	*11.00*	
Repairs	*35.00*	
Licensing	*47.50*	
		173.50
Insurance		
Health	*N/A*	
Life	*N/A*	
Automobile	*103.00*	
Homeowner's	*79.40*	
		182.40
Food		300.00
Household Items		44.00
Books, Movies, Restaurants		45.00
Professional Expenses		
Postage	*12.00*	
Telephone	*75.00*	
Office Supplies	*10.00*	
Memberships & Subscriptions	*22.00*	
		179.00
Incidental		60.00
Grand Total:		**$2,489.00**

In Figure 6-1, the Health and Life Insurance lines assume that you have those fully covered as a job benefit.

Now let's look at your new budget when you switch to writing full-time at home:

Figure 6-2. New Monthly Budget (as a Freelancer)

Category	Subcategory		Totals
Housing			
	Rent or House Payment	759.26	
	Incidental and Improvements	90.00	
			849.26
Telephone			75.00
Utilities			
	Gas & Electric	225.00	
	Water	72.00	
			297.00
Car Payments			323.84
Car Expense			
	Gasoline	24.00	
	Parking	0.00	
	Repairs	15.00	
	Licensing	47.50	
			86.50
Insurance			
	Health	220.00	
	Life	100.00	
	Automobile	103.00	
	Homeowner's	79.40	
			502.40
Food			300.00
Household items			44.00
Books, movies, restaurants			85.00
Professional expenses			
	Postage	18.00	
	Telephone	126.00	
	Office Supplies	35.00	
	Memberships & subscriptions	42.00	
			281.00
Incidental			60.00
Grand Total:			**$2,904.00**

An Unaffordable Amusement

I don't want to take up literature in a money-making spirit, or be very anxious about making large profits, but selling it at a loss is another thing altogether, and an amusement I cannot well afford.

—Lewis Carroll

As a freelance writer, at least in my experience, your automobile expenses are likely to go down (so long as you don't travel much for research purposes). Postage remains the same. Office supplies, membership and subscriptions, and legal and professional fees rise.

Also, you may now end up paying for all of your health insurance. Yes, the cost is absurd, and will only increase. (If you're lucky, you may be eligible to be included in your spouse's plan, but still there may be additional costs.)

As a freelancer, your new working budget is $2,904 monthly (not including taxes). This totals $34,848 per year. The roughly 15 percent increase in basic expenses ($415 per month) is mostly due to the costs of covering your own health and life insurance, along with some extra costs for telephone, professional fees, etc.

However, you also need to add in your tax burden, since now these deductions will not be subtracted directly from your take-home paycheck by your employer. Instead, you will get checks for your writing from publishers, and then you are responsible for paying your own income taxes, and your own Social Security taxes.

As a very broad approximation, let's estimate the tax on your gross income (after legitimate deductions) to be $5,200. When added to the $34,848 needed to cover your actual living expenses, this now takes us up to $40,048 per year. Let's call that an even $40,000.

In other words, to keep up your current lifestyle (in this example), your goal of gross annual receipts to bring in as a full-time writer is $40,000.

Income Projections: How Accurate?

You will want to set your own budget, following the rough categories I've laid out. Be sure to accurately calculate your actual housing expenses (or share of them, if you are splitting the costs with a spouse or partner who also brings in a paycheck.

After several years, of course, you will be able to refine your projections, even taking into account the cyclical nature of freelance writing and the publishing industry's needs.

For the purposes of discussion, however, let's stick with this tentative target of $40,000 to earn.

How will you do this? Here are a couple of possible approaches:

Figure 6-3. Possible Income Scenarios

Scenario 1

$20,000	advances (for 2 books)
$20,400	payments for 2 magazine columns ($850/column per month x 24)
$ 4,000	payments for 12 articles (varying payments, ave. $330 each)

$40,000

Scenario 2

$20,000	advances (for 2 books)
$20,000	payments for 50 articles (just about 1/week for 50 weeks; varying payments averaging $400/article)

$40,000

As you can see, there are any number of combinations that add up to the income goal we've set. The question: Which is the most realistic for you, given your actual connections, experience, subject areas, and so on?

For me, writing columns is something I enjoy doing; I enjoy

the monthly schedule and the style of columns—providing useful information, often in a personal, conversational style. And I have the connections and the experience to have secured these two lucrative, regular gigs.

You will note that these budgets do not include much royalty income from past books. The reason is that as you start out, you likely don't have many past books in print to earn residual royalties, after the advances are earned back. For that reason, I've focused on advances. However, over time, writing books that prove successful and stay in print can lead to some nice royalty checks that can do a lot to push future income projections higher than the $40,000 we've set as the initial target.

I believe anyone can write two books per year. But perhaps you cannot. In that case, can you hope for twice as large an advance for one book? No, the reality is that your advances will at first be small, until you can work your way up to commanding $20,000 advances—and writing successful books that sell well and recover that advance handily.

Maybe you can increase your income by selling articles to higher-paying magazines. Rather than $300 to $500 per article, can you line up assignments with magazines that pay $1,000 to $1,500 per article? That would be one way to make up the shortfall.

But can you really count on selling enough articles at those rates until you are an established contributor to those magazines? Perhaps. But it is more likely that you'll sell only a few articles at higher rates—if any. After all, there's much stiffer competition at that level. You'll do better at first to work harder, and plan to write more articles at the lower rates.

I don't mean to be discouraging, but you need to learn to think realistically when it comes to financial planning—especially for the first year of writing freelance full-time.

You discover soon enough that promises fade, and prospects recede. You can plan on doing more work than you estimate.

And don't count on anything. In fact, you should put this sign above your desk:

Don't count on anything
until the check is in your hands!

Contracts can disappear, assignments can be canceled, and royalties can vanish in the name of "reserve against returns." Inaccurate royalty accounting can diminish your cash income, too. Book and magazine publishers can go out of business, or file for bankruptcy. Your editor can be replaced by someone who doesn't want to work with you.

The scenarios are endless. The end result is the same: Your projections are reduced to molten slag by the lightning bolt of unfortunate reality.

When an event like this hits, you'll learn how good you are at damage control. "Will the freelancer net a book contract or magazine assignment to replace the lost income, and in time to save the ranch? Tune in next week at this time for another episode of *Write for Your Life!*"

Covering Your Bets

What if that big deal you're working on or awaiting really does fizzle?

I advise that you work to line up a replacement deal before you are forced to do it.

Even if you have a bird in hand, keep trying to catch those two in the bush. If none of them come through (very unlikely), it's time to scramble. If all come through (slightly unlikely), you'll just have to put in a lot more time at the keyboard. Or find a writer friend to take one over entirely, or help with one of the assignments. Chances are the favor will be returned in time.

Ever Hopeful

[A freelance writer is:] One who gets paid per word, per piece, or perhaps.
—Robert Benchley, humorist, quoted in Selected Letters of James Thurber, edited by H. Thurber and J. Weeks, 1981

Preparing for Rainy Days

Contingency Reserves

Cash-flow management involves looking ahead. But you cannot always foretell the future accurately, so you need to build flexibility into your budget.

Start by adding 10 to 20 percent to your budget estimates for expenses.

And decrease your anticipated income by a similar percent.

That way, you won't be surprised by hidden expenses, by diminished or delayed payments, or worst of all, deadbeat clients.

The best way to prepare for financial rainy days is to have a goodly amount of cash set aside to see you through a month or two of low income.

Note: I did not include any amount for savings in either of the bare-bones sample budgets given at the beginning of this chapter. But haven't you been saving money in preparation for becoming a full-time writer? And won't you try to continue adding to your savings on a regular basis when you are freelancing?

It needs to become a regular habit. When you get a check for an article or a book, take a certain percentage—even if it's a small one—and put it right into savings.

And you'll need to plan for seasonal variations in your annual income patterns. Even before I started writing full-time, I noticed a distinct shortage of writing income each January and February. And sure enough, the pattern carried over to my full-time career. The reason seems to be that publishing acquisitions slow down as they approach the Thanksgiving holiday. Editors frequently repeat that holiday mantra: "After the first of the year." Because of that, I always try to line up extra work in October and November.

Most years, I also saw a shortage in May. So I also start looking for additional work in March, to get me through the end of Spring.

You'll probably have at least one tight month, yourself. However you can, pare your general budget back as much as is practical. A leaner budget can absorb financial hits the first year or two, until you learn to even things out and become a more efficient and better-paid writer.

Taking Hits

Ask any writer. The tales of woe are endless. The following scenarios are ones I've lived through myself; they are typical of the disasters that can strike any working writer over the years.

- In 1990, I returned a signed contract to an arm of Prentice Hall and, with a deep sigh of relief, sat back to await the first $7,500 advance. Two weeks later I telephoned my editor. The company had decided to kill the entire line—a few days after I sent my signed contract back. No, I never got my check. The editor wasn't pleased; he had to phone over 90 other writers, tell them their contracts were canceled, and ask for their advance money to be returned.

- In 1983, the publisher of a magazine called *Softalk* filed for bankruptcy. As an unsecured creditor, I suspected I'd never get the money owed me, a bit over $900. Still, every couple of years, I would get a form from a bankruptcy court in Southern California asking if I wanted to remain part of the pending bankruptcy settlement. Dutifully, I signed the forms and returned them in postage-paid envelopes. In 1993, I received a check for $400—less than half of the money originally promised. And 11 years late.

- In the late 1980s and early 1990s, I had all my eggs in one basket—Simon & Schuster. This proved, at times, to be a pleasant relationship—except at royalty time. For whatever reasons, S&S had placed the responsibility for author royalty accounting and payment for all their publishing divisions in the hands of Prentice Hall. This should have worked fine, but it didn't. By some cosmic coincidence, Prentice Hall invariably happened to be "having problems with our new accounting software" every March and September, right at royalty time. This introduced more than a few errors, and royalty payments were usually delayed.

Trimming Expenses

Consider ways that you can be frugal with your business expenses—within reason. Can you get a better deal on your Internet service? What about telephone services? Do you really need caller ID? Can you get a better long-distance rate? Or—better than a lower rate—do you really need to make every long-distance call you place?

Do you really have to replace your computer now? If it's working, keep it awhile longer. (At least until the end of the year, to see whether you need the expense to reduce your taxes.)

Do you need big stacks of pre-printed letterhead paper? You can print a letterhead with your ink-jet or laser printer every time you print a letter. Likewise, you can also print business cards in small batches.

Those are but a few ideas. Success in managing cash-flow comes from two principles: (1) maximizing income and increasing its speed of arrival; and (2) shrinking or delaying the outflow of cash. Always ask yourself: Do I need it? And how soon? Can I postpone the purchase?

Establishing Credit

Credit is offered in various ways. Used properly, it can help you manage certain parts of your budget—such as expenses that must be paid before certain income comes in. But credit always comes at a cost. Credit cards are the most accessible—but also the most dangerous; the cost of missing a payment due date or running an unpaid balance is quite severe. Avoid having more than two or three, if that—and pay off any balance promptly each month.

Personally, I think it's wise to avoid maxing out any potential loan against your home equity. I find this is an important backup resource best saved for real emergencies.

And if you do have any consumer loans or major payments,

A Nice Savings on Auto Insurance

Let your auto insurance agent know that you will not be commuting to work. You may get a break on your car insurance.

I get a 10 percent discount, since I drive less than 20,000 miles per year, including "pleasure driving." (Pleasure driving is anything not work- or business-related.)

Of course, if you drive a lot doing research, interviews, or other writing-related work, you should count that mileage when you answer the insurance agent's question about the number of miles you drive per year.

make extra payments whenever you can. That "saves up" the money, and if you need to weather a brief financial storm, you can selectively miss a payment for a month or two.

Selling Yourself to Your Banker as a Business

It's a good idea to let your banker in on your plans. Make an appointment, take in some of your best article clippings or published books, along with check stubs, contracts, tax returns, and related documents.

The goal is to prove that you have been operating as a professional writer for some time. You want to establish yourself as a small business. Explain to the banker how publishing operates, show how much positive cash-flow you have enjoyed, and discuss your projections for the future.

The purpose: to request setting up a fast, inexpensive line of credit to use when money is scarce. The first few years I was writing, this came in very handy a number of times, such as in cases where I had gotten a new book contract, but cash on-hand was getting tight.

Rather than wait three or five weeks for the check, I would take the signed contract to the bank and get a loan of a few thousand dollars, based directly on the anticipated advance. This would be a 30- or 90-day note, with a set amount of interest. Why? Because this incurred less interest than a credit card cash advance—and required less tangible collateral than a consumer loan.

I never had a problem getting such a loan. The bank recognized me as a legitimate small business, and knew that the income to repay the loan was forthcoming.

Back-Up Plans

Another way to fill in the lean times is to seek some outside income. You might do this by finding a regular writing gig—still freelance, but regular—such as a magazine column. If you can't land one right away (and don't feel bad if you can't), you might try to land a contract to write a newsletter for a business or organization.

I did a number of what I call "hometown" writing jobs during my first ten years as a freelancer. Among them were:

- Writing form letters for businesses to use in soliciting business from consumers, established businesses, and new businesses.

- Editing and improving grant proposals. Museums, hospitals, university departments, tenured university faculty, college students, and practicing professionals are among your best potential customers. Grant proposals almost always need touching up for writing effectiveness and content organization.

- Covering political and organizations' meetings for the local weekly paper. (These get pretty boring, so the turnover is high among reporters for such events. You may not find it difficult to get such assignments on a regular basis.)

There are other (more lucrative) potential income sources, and we'll get into those in Chapter 10.

Keeping a Hand in the Working World

It doesn't hurt to stay in touch with what you used to do for a living, just in case you need extra money regularly for a while. Knowing it's only temporary work makes it easier.

When I first left my job of eight years, I contracted to do some work for my former boss, Don. He had started his own business on the side, involving something I had done in my old job (installing and repairing electronic liquor dispensers).

I wasn't desperate for money at the time, but Don didn't have anyone else who knew the equipment. It was a goodwill gesture, but it wasn't hard to take the extra checks, either. And it eased my worry that if I couldn't hack it writing full-time, getting a regular job would be easy.

So don't burn any bridges when you leave your old job. You may just need some fill-in work at some point. (And you might also consider staying in touch with any competitors your old employer might have.)

Intermittent Part-Time Employment

If things do slow down enough to require that you seek outside work, consider a part-time job. In the mid-1990s, I experienced a slump in my writing income, and had just moved to a new town. At the urging of my partner at the time, I decided to pick up a regular job for a few hours a week.

I am a "motorhead" and enjoy classic cars (at the time, I owned a 1967 Dodge). So I applied for a job as a counterman at an auto parts store. I'd never done that sort of work, but I figured I could hand out parts easily enough.

Besides the money, I benefited greatly from getting out of the house. I got to know more people in the new town faster. I really enjoyed the work—and even got a couple of great articles out of the advice I handed out freely with the parts.

It really does make self-employment a little less stressful to know that you have a good budget, the foresightedness and determination to manage your money well . . . and a fallback option or two to see you through any unexpected bumps in the road.

Fear Breeds Respect and Caution

So, you are ready to quit your job next week to write full-time. How do you feel? Scared? Confident? Cocky?

Ideally, you will accept the responsibility you've taken on, no matter how things turn out, and be prepared to accept setbacks as well as success.

You should feel some apprehension. If you know that you will succeed grandly in everything you do, you may be setting yourself up for a fall. Too much cockiness, and you may ignore signals that you need to change something before you fail.

I'm reminded of a country/pop crossover song from the 1980s, titled "Love Will Get You Through Times of No Money (Better Than Money Will Get You Through Times of No Love)." That's a nice sentiment, but doesn't go very far when yours is the primary income in a household. Let's face it. All the love in the world won't pay the bills.

If the bills go unpaid long enough, you'll find yourself facing one hell of a distraction—perhaps enough to knock you out of freelancing for good.

A little fear is a good thing. A guy named Jerry Creelman, who was my scuba instructor in 1971, worked hard to generate fear in new divers. He spent a lot of classroom time on the dangers of the sport. He had gruesome photos of accidents—divers torn open by boat props, demolition caused by not treating a 2,250-psi tank with respect, drowning victims recovered days after they got into trouble 90 feet down, that sort of thing.

He also had his own equally frightful tales to tell—blowing out a lung, running out of air at the wrong time, getting the bends. I remember thinking, Right—I'm taking this stuff seriously! Creelman taught divers to fear the water, because if you fear something, you'll respect it and won't be careless.

So, for the first few years of full-time writing, respect the professional and financial dangers around you. And you need to continue to show care throughout your career. I know of several writers who grew too complacent, lived at the edge of their incomes, and believed falsely that the money would always be there.

Keeping Score?

How do you define and measure success?

Success is often defined as meeting goals. If you write full-time, will you measure your success by your income? Or will you strive to write a certain number of books or articles each year?

Measuring your success by goals like these is okay—to a point. They are motivators, and allow you to gauge progress. But do they truly tell you how well you are doing? The danger is that the first time you fail to achieve a goal, you may feel a sense of failure. You may believe you are a "poor" writer—not just in financial terms, but in writing ability.

But in the writing field, we all experience some failure. And writing ability, or lack thereof, is frequently not the cause of it. In fact, occasional failure may be needed in order to grow to be a successful writer.

Consider the careers of many major writers. Herman Melville's just one example. After surviving capture by Polynesian natives, Melville wrote his first book, *Typee*, based on that experience. It was tremendously successful, and Melville took up writing full-time for the next six years, enjoying success from several books. But when his novel *Moby Dick* was published in 1851, it received no critical acclaim, and made little money. Two novels before that had met the same fate.

Discouraged, Melville turned to farming to support his family, and wrote a few short stories on the side. He was convinced that his career as a full-time writer was over. He traveled one last

Crash!

I have made a good living by writing, earning over $65,000 most years, with a high point of $90,000 one year.

But the year after that $90K year, I found myself running out of work. And a series of family and marital problems left me unable to work at times.

In fact, the following year I worked only six months. But even then I grossed $47,000. That wasn't bad for what was essentially half a year's work. And I had a growing shelf full of books I'd written, offering some validation of my work.

But I was unhappy. Part of the problem: I had tied my sense of self-worth to how well I was doing financially. I felt that I had to outdo myself every year, and if I didn't I was failing.

It took a while, but I eventually realized what I was doing. Now I try to focus more on working—and less on worrying that I'm not measuring up to a recent accomplishment or high-water mark.

The results are better in the long run.

time to Europe in 1857 to visit his friend, writer Nathaniel Hawthorne, and returned home still unknown. He got a job as a customs inspector, and worked at that until his death at age 72, twenty years later. His importance as a great American literary figure was not recognized until the 20th century.

Your career needs to be rooted in solid, well-planned goals. Think about how you will measure your success. Then develop a plan that will take you steadily there, step by step.

And don't confuse measuring your self-worth with measuring your writing success.

CHAPTER 7

Making the Break

YOU'VE DONE YOUR CALCULATIONS and planned and mapped out the route. What do you do next? You can continue to prepare and put off the decision—for years, if you wish. But if you want and truly need to become a full-time writer, chances are you will not do it if you wait too long. Now is the time.

But don't jump into this today (not literally, at least)! I want you to stand back and double-check your situation.

Decision or Delusion?

- Are you truly at the point where, if you had twice as much time for writing as you do now, you could line up enough paying work to keep you busy for six months?

- Do your writing credits include two or more books (either finished and published, or under contract)? Or have you published more than a few magazine pieces? (A good target is at least 15 per year over the past three years.)

- For two consecutive years, have you earned at least half as much as you need to live on by writing part-time?

- Are you confident that you can exercise self-discipline and self-motivation when needed?

- Have you published in more than one field or category of writing?

- Are you willing to make changes in your work when an editor asks—or do you argue for every word and punctuation mark?

- If it proved necessary, would you accept having to work full-time again? Or part-time?

One final question. After you read and consider your responses: Are you being honest with yourself? It is easy to gloss things over and say you are prepared, when you are not. Be certain that it is not simply your desire to write for a living that responded to any of those questions.

As I have said, there really is no way to quantify your readiness to write full-time. The truth rests in the details of your skills, your situation, and your possibilities. But these are the questions you must ask, and be confident in the direction your answers indicate. Consider your responses, change them as necessary on second look, and see how you feel.

Please don't lie to yourself. If you feel that one or another of your honest responses shows a weakness, re-evaluate everything. If your gut instinct tells you "No," you may be better off to wait a few months, at least. In the meantime, work on improving those deficient area(s). And keep drawing your steady paycheck from your regular job. You'll be doing yourself a big favor.

Sharing the Decision

First and foremost, consider your spouse or partner. She or he lives with you and will share in the events and emotional ups and downs of your career, both good and bad. And if your partner depends on you for even a bit of financial support, the roller-coaster ride of a writer's early career as a full-time freelancer can take its toll on both of you.

It's your life. You will make the ultimate decision, but give this significant person a chance for advice and other input.

You may also want to share your goals with a good friend or two. They will have an excellent view of you and your work from the outside. And if they are anything like my friends, they will tell you straight-up what they think. Listen carefully to any advice they may offer.

As for your extended family outside your home, I will say this: If they can't perceive the part-time writing you do now as legitimate professional work, I can almost guarantee that you will get little support for your goal of taking it on full-time. Still, think about specific areas they can help you with—small business advice, professional services they can recommend, or even potential customers for your writing.

What about your children? Certainly you must tell them what you are doing, and explain that you will be home most of the time to do your work. Consider, and share with them, what minor (or major) changes this might effect in their routines. For example, because you will be up against tight deadlines and sometimes will need to stay up late or work a little on weekends, you may have to miss a few appointments, sporting events, recitals, or other things on occasion. But also, there will be times (when you are not facing a strict deadline) when you will have more personal freedom and be able to choose to do some special things with them that you couldn't before.

You might begin to make your children familiar with the term "deadline" and how important deadlines are for your career. It's a concept you'll want them to understand and respect, especially the next time you have to say, sorry, I can't do that tomorrow, I've got a deadline I need to meet.

The Time Has Come

There is one thing stronger than all the armies in the world, and that is an idea whose time has come.
—Victor Hugo

Advice or Encouragement?

When you share your decision with others, you will get advice—even if you do not ask for it. Some of it will be contrary to what you yourself think is the best course of action.

Some may be jealous of you and your (imagined) new freedom, and that will affect their reactions and advice. But most advice you get will be given with good intent. Some may try to discourage you. One or two might give you absurd advice. (I remember my father telling me, "If you can make that much money writing full-time, why not keep your job and write that much on the side?")

No matter how you feel about the advice, or how little sense it makes, accept it politely. Sort out what's useful later, in private. If you try to argue with friends or family, you can end up in an unhappy disagreement that can linger for years, to no one's benefit. You'll do better to avoid such distractions.

Yes, you will get some discouraging advice. Some of it could be worth considering. At best, you might hear a comment or tip from someone that gets you thinking about ways to make the switch even more successfully. In any case, if you ask for advice, be ready to accept discouragement as well as encouragement.

Remember: Becoming a full-time writer is moving into a real career. Always keep this in mind: You are moving up. Thinking otherwise can bring self-doubt.

Breaking the News to Your Boss

When you inform your employer, treat your move as if you are leaving one job for another. You may get some ridicule, or complete incredulity. As with anything else, the right attitude goes a long way toward avoiding conflict and a rising blood pressure.

Don't burn your bridges. Perhaps you are thinking, "Why do I need to give my boss any consideration in this?" But remember: You may need to return to your old job some day.

As distasteful as that prospect may be, keep this option open. Even if the atavistic fool deserves no notice at all, grit your teeth and be polite—or at least reasonable. Leaving on good terms will grease the rails for you to return, should the need arise.

And you might want to stay in touch with the old crowd at work. You'll have valuable information if you find yourself job-hunting down the road—whether seeking a job with your old employer, or with the employer's competition. And you may get to hear just how important you were at your job. I visited my old place of employment two months after I left. I couldn't help but be mildly gratified to see that things were in a mess, and that it took 1.5 people to do my former job.

I do realize that some people can make it really tough on you for the last couple of days or weeks before you leave. But be polite, and be sure to give proper notice.

In some situations, in particular, you must give a certain amount of notice in order to switch over retirement or insurance or stock programs. Be sure to study the fine print in any policies or benefit programs to make sure you are proceeding in a way that will not jeopardize separation or continuation benefits to which you are entitled.

Leaving Your Job

Although some employee benefits are shrinking in today's economic climate, you will likely have some benefits that are due you. These may include stock or profit-sharing programs, a retirement program, and possibly others.

More Planning Ahead

In the months before I left my job to write full-time, I did a number of things in preparation.

Because I had exceptional medical-dental coverage, I was able to schedule some important oral surgery. That allowed me to recover with sick-leave pay, and to get the surgery out of the way. And I knew I couldn't afford the time to stay in bed recovering after I began to write as a full-time freelancer.

While I had my job, I also bought a new car and got an extra credit card (for cash reserve). I thought it would be better to get those things done while my credit rating was still strong.

At the earliest appropriate time, visit your company's human resources department. Advise them of your intent to take up writing full-time, and discuss what options are available either to continue a given benefit—or perhaps to "cash out" an accumulated benefit, such as unused sick leave or vacation time.

Employer-funded retirement programs sometimes offer the choice to continue or cash out your account. When I left my job to write, I was vested in a company retirement program. I elected to leave the money where it was. Two years later, I was surprised to receive a large check in the mail. As it turned out, my state of residence had new legislation that required some retirement programs to cash out participants under certain circumstances.

If you participate in a stock-purchase or option plan, find out what you need to do to derive maximum benefit from the plan. You may want to work out the quarter, the year, or a fiscal year to obtain the greatest benefit.

Health insurance is vital. If you have coverage through your employer's group plan, inquire about the costs and procedures involved to let you continue your coverage. This option, referred to by its acronym of COBRA, allows you to continue your coverage (but at your expense) for a time after you leave your job. It's usually less expensive than buying health insurance outright.

Also, ask whether a Certificate of Insurance is offered and required in your state. This certifies that you have been insured for however many years, which helps insurance companies determine if they want to keep you enrolled or not, and it may reduce your cost, as well.

You will eventually have to buy health insurance. If you're relatively young, healthy, and single, you may get by with a few hundred dollars per month, depending on where you live. If you have a spouse and children to cover, it will cost a great deal more. (I recently checked the cost of health insurance for a family with two children, and found that coverage (with an 80 percent co-pay) was $6,000 or more per year.

You can often do better than this by buying coverage through a plan or plans offered by professional organizations. Contact the organizations listed in Appendix A and ask them about any group health plans they might offer as benefits to their members.

Establishing New Business Accounts

You will find it easier to deal with some service and/or supplies vendors if you promptly establish yourself as a small business. For example, Federal Express makes it easy for you to set up a charge account under a business name. They'll even supply you with preprinted labels. Pay 'em promptly when the bills come, and you're in business.

For several years, I had all of my writing and computer supplies delivered by a small chain called Microcenter. Even with UPS charges, it cost less than shopping locally. To set up any such accounts, you just need an address, phone number, and business name. ("Michael Banks Associates" always worked for me.)

Some suppliers may request that you be personally responsible and will do a personal credit check. You can start out that way. Then, a year later, request that your business name be the only entity attached to your account. If you're lucky, the vendor will agree (you might suggest that you are looking at other potential vendors). After that, if they report to a major credit bureau, it will further bolster your business identity—provided that you do pay your bills promptly within 30 days.

Bargaining for Discounts

With some vendors, I eventually found that I could bargain for lower prices on supplies, services, and even equipment. In most cases, I had to agree to spend some minimum dollar amount with that vendor each year. That was usually no more than the amount of what I bought, anyway, and often was less.

Sometimes a discount is there for the asking. Quite a few businesses have a standard, scaled discount they will give you if you simply ask about their discounts for small businesses. It never hurts to mention that you are shopping around for the best rates.

Also, some discounts are available if you are a member of a professional organization. See Appendix A for organizations which offer such benefits.

Libel Insurance

If there is some aspect about a book or article that you're contemplating that may be a potential source of litigation involving accusations of libel, you may wish to consider insurance to protect you against such claims.

There are policies that protect writers against claims of libel, slander, invasion of privacy, and copyright infringement. Typical coverage includes written and spoken material, plus Internet-related claims. Sometimes these policies are available through national writers' organization, which in turn make arrangements through commercial insurance companies.

The best approach though, is being thoroughly accurate, reasonably cautious, and sticking to the facts when writing about controversial topics.

Incorporation

You may want to look into incorporation. As a corporation, your personal assets are protected if there is a judgment against you involving your work. The judgment is rendered against the corporation, rather than the individual writer.

The type of incorporation that many writers use is called a "Subchapter 'S'" corporation. This type of corporation accommodates sole proprietors very nicely, because no taxes are levied on the corporation; instead, all income is passed on to the writer, who is liable for income tax.

You will want an attorney with experience in this area to file the paperwork for you. For basic information, see the instructions for IRS form 1120S.

Taxes for the Self-Employed Writer

This subject requires an entire book in itself, and I hesitate to give definitive instructions, since there is a risk they will change over time with new IRS procedures and interpretations.

For instance, recently the IRS determined that it was not sufficient to keep credit-card charge slips as evidence of travel and entertainment expenditures; instead, they require that you keep the original receipt from the business (since these source receipts probably itemize the charges more precisely).

In general, the first principle is to keep on top of things with good record-keeping. Keep all paperwork relating to income and especially for expenditures. Realize that it is not always clear to an outside auditor what you are buying and why it relates to your business. So the first thing is to keep every scrap of paper that indicates what something is.

The second principle is to make notes on those documents at the time of purchase to explain more clearly what that something is and why you needed it. If you are buying a reference book for a specific research project, for instance, note on the check or receipt what project you plan to use this for. If you get a receipt from a print shop for making multiple copies of your resume sheet, make a note of that fact on the receipt; otherwise, it just says, "Copies." Of what? an auditor may well ask.

The third principle is to file things well. As noted earlier, the system need not be complex; often the simpler the system, the easier it is to maintain and actually find things. Store your receipts by project (especially if you can bill a client for any of those costs, like express shipping, in addition to your basic fee), or by major vendor (your FedEx folder, for instance), or by type of expense (shipping and postage), or simply by month.

More Savings

Don't forget your quarterly estimated tax payments.

You can budget this easily. The amount you need to pay to avoid underpayment penalties is based on what you paid in taxes the preceding year. Request IRS Publication 505 for details.

Don't let this slip by you. It helps to open a savings account solely for tax payments, or to set up another short-term investment, to make sure that a payment is never missed due to a temporary lack of funds.

You can find a good overview of financial record-keeping for tax purposes at www.writing-world.com, in particular several excellent articles by Moira Allen, "The Taxman Cometh, Parts I and II." These articles include references to useful books and Web sites for the self-employed writer.

One of these useful publications is the *Writer's Pocket Tax Guide,* by attorney Darlene Cypser (www.foolscap-quill.com). This comprehensive publication, updated annually, is available as a CD-ROM. It covers the rules for depreciation, auto expenses, home-office deductions, and so on. It explains the various tax forms with line-by-line instructions, and includes the actual IRS tax forms and publications.

Pay Your Taxes Promptly!

You can get in a whole lot of financial trouble by not paying your taxes. The Internal Revenue Service levies stiff penalties, plus interest, on any money you owe. There may also be specific fines.

You can avoid all this by making sure your quarterly estimated tax payments come to at least 80 percent of your previous year's gross income. And pay any additional taxes you owe by April 15.

Also, remember that you will be paying double self-employment taxes, since you are now both employee and employer. See Form SE and its instructions at the IRS Web site, www.irs.gov.

If you get into tax trouble, whether with the IRS or with state or local tax agencies, find the money and pay the tax debt ASAP. This is an excellent time to tap into any emergency savings or line of credit. If you fall behind and don't do anything about it, the IRS or your state may start seizing things—your car, perhaps your house. An unpleasant prospect, indeed!

If you cannot pay the debt immediately, work out a payment arrangement with the IRS. Use a lawyer, or do it yourself if you feel confident. Make sure it's something you can live with, and in the meantime, be sure to keep up with your current taxes.

Again, it's best to avoid all of this. Find a good tax accountant (preferably local, as the national chain employees tend to come and go).

You may hear of great tax dodges. Don't believe 'em. The perennial "offshore banking" and similar scams pushed by con artists on the Internet and via U.S. mail and seminars are no way to reduce your taxes. They can't hide your money from the IRS; all they do is pad the pockets of scamsters with your hard-earned cash.

My Own Story: Making the Transition from Part-Time to Full-Time Writer

I've given you some background on how and why I made the switch to writing full-time. Here are more of the details.

After ten years of writing part-time, I had a strong desire to find more time for writing. I had one book in print, and a few hundred magazine credits. Plus, I had a contract for a second book in hand, and knew I could write a third book if I had the time.

But this was 1980, and I was married and had young children. Going full-time just did not seem a practical thing to do. Instead, I trimmed work and family duties just a bit, and slept less, to gain more time to write.

In two years, my writing was bringing in more than half of what I made at my job—and taking less than half the time. From somewhere there came the awareness that I might possibly be ready and able to make it as a full-time writer. After all, I figured my writing income might double if I went full-time. This meant I would net more than my salary.

Thus, I had the means—a proven way to make a decent income. And the motivations were there: greater personal freedom, more money, more time to write.

All I lacked was opportunity—a good set of circumstances for the transition. I started thinking more seriously about how to go about writing for a living. (I also increased my regular savings account deposits.)

Opportunity came in the form of some oral surgery that required my taking two weeks off work. A couple days after the surgery, on a Monday, I became a full-time writer.

That is, I wrote daily, and sought new opportunities and assignments. While recovering at home from the surgery, I wrote most of the day, and late at night. It was exhilarating. I was in control of my schedule. No more pager to disrupt my life, no rushing into the plant or to a customer site every morning.

Hey, I thought, I can live like this! I extended my sabbatical by adding on a vacation week. Meanwhile, I wrote and lined up more work.

Came the Monday I was to return to work—well, I didn't. I was a full-time writer. My alarm went off Monday morning, because I decided the best way to start the first day was to have to do something. That something was an interview with the manager and tour of a Voice of America relay station. I had an assignment to write a piece on it for a new magazine.

It was a long drive to reach the site of the interview. In fact, I realized I was getting up nearly as early as I used to for my old job. (But to make up for it, I've slept in for something like 6,000 mornings since.)

Still, it proved a good idea. When I awoke, I "went to work" as if I was at any other job. That set the tone for the week, the month, and for many more years.

Thus began my writing career. After a trial run, I jumped right into it with both feet! I've never looked back.

CHAPTER 8

Marketing Tips & Techniques

FREEDOM! IT'S THE FIRST DAY of the first week of your writing career. You're up and typing furiously at the keyboard. Or you're sitting behind the wheel of your car on your way to do some research, or perhaps to conduct an interview.

Or are you? Perhaps you're thinking you might prefer to meditate beside a stream in a nearby park. Or maybe spend the afternoon window-shopping.

Why? Because you can.

You are your own boss and can do anything you want.

Just remember: You're at a new job; you didn't retire. Keeping this job requires that you work, as does any job.

And one key task may be one at which, as a part-time writer, you didn't need to work quite as seriously. That's the field of marketing.

Marketing your writings will be a crucial factor—perhaps *the* crucial factor—in your success. You may not yet be able to do it perfectly, but you had better learn quickly how to do it regularly and methodically.

Otherwise, you may be back searching the want ads, looking for a job in the 9 to 5 workplace, sooner than you think.

Schedule Time for Marketing

So before you do anything else, sit down with your schedule. And if you haven't already, block off time to spend on market research and actual marketing (sending queries, etc.).

If you already have some time slots for that lined up on your work calendar, ask yourself: Is it enough? Do I have enough paying assignments lined up for the next few weeks? For the next three months? The next half year?

Or longer? And what happens if a key project falls through; do you have a back-up project cooking on a slow burner? If not—you need to increase your marketing time.

Not later.

Now.

For many of you, writing may be the easy part—even if it seems the most tortuous, because you agonize over it and stay up late to write until you're bleary-eyed. But what separates the successful writers from the rest is the ability to write *and* to sell.

Take marketing seriously, by devoting significant time to it, and you are more likely to succeed. So make sure you're putting in the time to find new markets and to make sure old markets for your work know what you'd like to write for them next.

Finding Markets for Your Work

As a full-time writer, well-paying markets—particularly repeat or regular ones—are critical to your success. After all, you are writing to be published and paid for it.

Whether you are writing full- or part-time, you should at least take the time to look through the market listings in *The*

Writer and *Writer's Digest* every month. But monthly market listings are only the beginning.

What other resources are there, beyond the writers' magazines? Well, lots of them. They include trade journals, annual directories of publishers and their personnel, information about publishers in general-interest magazines and news sources, and writers' organizations.

There are small-press magazines that cater to readers and writers of specific genres. There are publishers' catalogs.

Web sites for writers often provide market info. If that's not enough, networking with your peers can be excellent sources for market news.

Finally, you can get information by studying the products themselves—the books and magazines created by publishers in your field of interest. You can learn a lot by studying the selection found at your favorite local bookstores.

Let's have a look at what's out there for you, and how to get at it.

Web Sites for Writers

Web sites for writers number well into the hundreds. (See Appendix A for a list of some significant ones.) Some are free, some aren't. Some are sponsored by national writers' organizations (such as ASJA) and have members-only resources. Some sponsor workshops and critiques. Nearly all list markets for freelancers, and a few carry news of the publishing world.

In addition, such sites offer opportunities for networking with other writers and exchanging gossip.

My favorite Web sites offer at least two of these elements:

- Market information and publishing news

- Discussion forums or bulletin boards

- Articles by or interviews with professional writers or editors

As you may imagine, I am rather demanding about market news; I want to see info on paying markets.

The Writers Write Web site (http://www.writerswrite.com) does an excellent job of providing market info via searchable databases. The site also has publishing news. It hosts worthwhile discussion forums and features some useful how-to articles.

The Market List (http://www.marketlist.com) is a good site for genre fiction writers. Semi-pro as well as professional markets are listed, and you will find news here you can't find anywhere else. Searchable market listings are available, and the site offers archives of editor and author interviews.

The Mining Co. offers a Web site for freelance writers (http://freelancewrite.miningco.com) with excellent articles and a good selection of market listings. This site also delves into specialized writing areas, such as technical writing, PR, greeting cards, and grant writing.

Finally, there are Web sites for the writer magazines, such as *The Writer* (http://www.writermag.com) and *Writer's Digest* (http://www.writersdigest.com).

Literary Market Place: The Bible of the Publishing Industry

Every category of industry or business has its "Bible"—a comprehensive directory of companies in the field, often including related businesses. Among book publishers and editors, this tome is called *Literary Market Place* (commonly known as *LMP*).

LMP is a massive book (with more than 1,500 pages). With other content, it lists book publishers and their staff, with titles. This is the sort of detailed information writers submitting their own work really need, such as which specific editor is responsible for which particular categories. Agents know the value of keeping up with this information, so book proposals are sent to the right person. Using *LMP*, you can too.

The book also lists agents, fellowships and grants, and associations.

If you are promoting a book, there are listings of book reviewers, and means of getting reviews and publicity in radio, television, and other media. *LMP* also lists magazines focused on the publishing trade, along with literary events and awards, and more.

I used to buy my own copy each year, but when the price went over $200, I turned to the public library. (*LMP*'s price is now over $300.)

There is an online version of *LMP* at http://www.literary-marketplace.com/.

Magazines & Journals for Writers

There is a variety of journals specifically for writers and publishers. As mentioned, you can find them listed in *LMP* (under the heading "Magazines for the Trade"), in *The Writer's Handbook* ("Writing & Publishing"), and in *Writer's Market* ("Journalism & Writing").

These magazines for writers include *The Writer*, *Canadian Writer's Journal*, and *Writer's Digest* for freelancers, and *American Journalism Review*, *Editor & Publisher*, and *Publishers Weekly* for writers employed in the publishing trade.

Any of these can be excellent sources on publishing in general, as well as offering news and features about specific companies. There are also some very specialized journals focusing on one segment of publishing, such as *Copy Editor* and *Ohio Writer*.

Publisher News

There are several ways to find out what's happening at a specific publishing house. The first is to visit the publisher's Web site. You can see what's being published and pushed, as well as what's coming up in the near future. In addition, you can find writers' submission guidelines.

Press releases are another good way to get information. Like most companies, book and magazine publishers issue a lot of press releases. You can usually get on the list by sending a request to the publisher's publicity or marketing department. Once you're on the list, you won't be dropped for a few years. (To stay on the list, occasionally mention the publisher's books or magazines in an article, or review a book. Then send a copy of the write-up to the publicity person.)

You should definitely request publishers' catalogs, which are always revealing resources. They tell and show you what a publisher is publishing now—and the promotional copy tells why they think it will sell. If nothing else, they are great idea generators. If they are featuring an important new book on a subject, does that suggest to you a related proposal in which they might logically have an interest? I always keep a big collection of these catalogs in my marketing files, and look over each new one when it arrives, pen in hand, to jot down a slew of ideas that the catalog will surely generate.

Free books for possible review? Well, it depends on the publisher, the publicity department's budget, and whether you regularly write reviews for consumer or trade publications. Do not ask for books for review unless you seriously intend to consider them, and really have a market to place a review.

Before you submit any proposals, you'll want to verify editor names and get their latest writers' guidelines. Often, these can be found on the Web. And you can look up the most recent published information on who's who at a publishing house in *LMP*. However, you'll still want to telephone or write to book publishers to verify the current person to whom you should submit your proposal, along with requesting the latest writers' guidelines. You may be surprised to discover that the information posted on the Web site isn't current, and that an editor has changed positions since the most recent edition of *LMP* was printed.

Some book and magazine publishers don't provide guidelines for writers. And some publishers—especially the larger book houses—make it almost impossible to reach an editor by telephone. (This is a reasonable defense for editors who otherwise would get so many calls from people who want to write books that it would leave little time for work.) Still, you can often call and get through to an editorial assistant who at least can confirm the correct person to send your proposal to. Don't talk their ear off or make a pitch on the phone. Just get the info and mail in your materials; that's the only way to get full consideration. And having the right editor's name on the manuscript prevents your manuscript from getting lost in the shuffle.

Bookstores as Sources of Market Information

First of all, bookstore chains and many independent bookstores offer free newsletters, sometimes little magazines, that you can pick up in the store. These vary in size and complexity, but all contain news of the latest books from publishers. Publishers pay for the space devoted to their books in these publications. As you might imagine, the books with the biggest write-ups and featured reviews represent what publishers are currently pushing.

Also, the checkout counters or bulletin boards often have leaflets about forthcoming books and info about upcoming author signings hosted by that store.

In addition, the bookstore staff (this is true also of library personnel) range from experts on the book publishing industry to couldn't-care-less sorts. Often, they include avid readers who follow a genre or a particular type of book closely. Chatting with the friendly workers at your favorite bookstore may lead to all sorts of useful inside information. It often happens that people who sell books are writers, too.

And often libraries and bookstores host writer group meetings and literary lectures of interest. And bookstore staff are often involved in picking favorite books that are featured as "staff picks." Getting to know a bookstore worker or two won't lead directly to your selling more work, but it is part of learning how the business operates—what buyers and their customers notice and value about books.

Magazine Web Sites

There are at least several thousand established magazines that have Web sites. (By "established" I mean print magazines that prospered before the Web.)

The information you can glean from a magazine's Web site can be very illuminating. There may be flash polls. If the magazine has a message system, you can, in effect, get reader reaction to specific issues' contents, as well as to the magazine's general direction. This info will usually represent a larger pool of readers than Letters to the Editor in the print version.

As mentioned, magazines often post their submission guidelines. A few also post the themes or focus of issues 6 to 12 months ahead. This gives you a tremendous edge, because you can submit material that fits the desired focus, increasing the likelihood of a sale dramatically.

Studying Magazine Markets

Studying magazine publishers involves more than simply reading an issue or two of a magazine. Once you really begin to track the work of a magazine, you begin to see a very clear picture of who their readers are, and how the editor(s) accommodate their needs.

The astute writer, interested in submitting work to a given publication, will take the time to read a good portion of the magazine, often scanning it from cover to cover. Of course, a few writers have submitted articles successfully to magazines they've never seen. But it's rare. To really find and connect with those magazines that might become long-term markets for your writing, you'll have to become more familiar with them.

Magazines generally offer four elements to study: content, editorials, advertising, and reader comments.

Content

A magazine's content is your primary guide to what an editor might buy. Examine several issues (I'd recommend three to five as a good number) to get an idea of the range of subjects the magazine features.

Look for slants the articles take. If the magazine runs articles on family life, does it address parents, or the entire family? If there are articles on auto racing, are they aimed at fans, at participants, or perhaps at race sponsors?

The content can also tell you things about the readership—your ultimate audience. What is the level of language used? What is the depth of coverage of topics? This can help you gauge the relative sophistication of the readership. So can the types of subjects covered, and the preferred styles. Are there more Q&A interviews than interview profiles? Do the articles tend to be round-ups, or in-depth coverage of one aspect of a subject?

If the magazine carries fiction,

Submission Guidelines

Printed submission guidelines usually provide the following:

• Focus/slant of the magazine, and information about its audience (often with demographic info)

• What type of material is accepted (feature articles, short pieces, essays, or fillers; book reviews; photos/illustrations/artwork; letters to the editor, etc.)

• Name of the editor(s) to whom work should be sent and address, phone, fax, and e-mail address

• Technical details of how to submit material (e.g., double-spaced, in Times 12pt, etc.)

On Web sites, editorial guidelines are usually listed under a heading like "Submission Guidelines," "Contributor Guidelines," or "Information for Authors."

If none of these choices appear, look for headings like "Contact Us" or "About Us." Some presses use a self-explanatory e-mail address like "queries@ourmag.com" or "submissions@ourmag.com." You can also check the site's map or index.

If you can't find guidelines, send an e-mail request for Author Guidelines to the editorial staff, or mail in your request with an SASE.

A word of caution: When you visit a magazine's Web site, be sure that you have found submission guidelines for the print magazine (assuming that is where you want your work published), and not the magazine's online version. A larger magazine may have a Web site that exists as a separate "publication" from the print version, perhaps with some unique content—and different submission guidelines, pay rates, and editors.

look for repeating elements in stories. Does the magazine favor a male or a female protagonist? Are the protagonists ordinary or extraordinary people? Are the endings usually downbeat or happy? Do you see stories heavy on dialogue, or on narrative and exposition?

One caveat: The issue of a magazine on the rack today was produced about three months ago. And the editor made the final decision on what the content would be four months back. In the interim, things can change. The magazine may change its slant—perhaps seeking to appeal to a more up-market audience. Or the editor may leave, with a new editorial direction coming in with the new personnel.

You likely won't discover such changes for a couple of months. Just take with a grain of salt what you read into issues, especially back issues. Treat it like a dated map for a busy highway that is constantly undergoing repairs and re-routing.

Keep your ears and eyes open for market news from other sources that might indicate where this potential publisher is headed in the near future.

Advertising

Advertising is often a good indicator of reader interests. Ads that do not work well do not run for very long. So it is usually safe to assume that any ad that runs more than three issues (the typical "test ad" run) is pulling responses. Therefore, it represents something that interests the magazine's readership. Any single ad doesn't represent the interests of all readers, but suggests there are enough of them to make it worthwhile to pay attention.

Thus, if a magazine carries a good number of ads for, let us say, fortune-tellers, Tarot cards, and books on the occult, you can figure that articles on those topics will be welcome. And you probably won't sell an article to the magazine debunking such things.

Not every ad will generate article ideas, and some ads are for things that readers enjoy but the magazine wouldn't touch, editorially. Still, it is worth looking at what readers are buying. With creative thinking, you can use magazine advertising to develop a fairly accurate profile of reader interests.

Editorials

If a magazine features a monthly message or commentary from the editor, read it carefully. It will give you some idea of how the editor thinks. And the editor is the first person you want to impress with your writing.

Most of us will never meet magazine editors to whom we sell (or want to sell). Editorials offer the closest thing to getting to know editors' public personas and personalities.

Editors also use editorials to signal important coming changes in their magazines. Also, it happens sometimes that an editor will invite input or even request manuscripts on a hot topic in an editorial.

Sample Issues

Many editors suggest, and for good reason, that you read at least one sample issue of their magazine or periodical before submitting any query or manuscript.

In fact, most feel strongly that you should not only read it, but study it to understand better their audience, style, and scope—before they take time out of their busy schedules to evaluate your proposed idea.

To get sample issues, call or write the editor of the magazine or the customer sales and service department of the publisher. Tell them that you are a writer and ask for a complimentary copy (along with writers' guidelines).

Many are willing to send you the most recent issue free of charge. Others may ask that you send an SASE along with the cover price of the magazine.

If your request falls upon deaf ears, you can always scout your local libraries, bookstores, newsstands, hobby shops, or specialty stores to find the publication(s) you are looking for.

Reader Comments

Along with ads, published reader comments are very helpful in building a profile of a magazine's readership. The majority of letters in a magazine's letter column are probably representative of the readership as a whole. This gives you a first-hand look at this target community that you hope will be interested in your writing.

Watch for reader polls, too. You won't see many, but take special note when one does appear.

Studying Book Publishers

Keep in mind that looking at recently published books generates some false impressions. Why? It all has to do with timing. Books released today (except those books that pop up instantly when someone like Elvis Presley dies) were contracted for one to two years before they reached the bookstores. In the interim, the publisher may have changed its line entirely. But once a book is in the production pipeline, very little can prevent its publication and distribution.

This means that judging a publisher's line by the books you see appearing on the market can leave you with information that is two years or more out of date. Just because you see a lot of romance novels from a given publisher in your local bookstore doesn't mean the publisher is buying romance novels now. So don't just submit your romance novel; it could prove to be a waste of time and money.

First, double-check these sources of information:

- *Book publisher catalogs.* These catalogs present their newest books, often forthcoming releases that won't appear in the bookstore for many months. They also list the most successful backlist books. Request catalogs directly from publishers. Large trade publishers may issue a catalog monthly, while most issue their catalogs two or three times a year, to coincide with the traditional publishing seasons (Fall and Spring are the biggest; some publishers have an extra Winter mini-season.)

- **Publishers Weekly** *magazine.* This is the most important trade magazine for the book publishing industry. It not only contains information about new and upcoming books and lines, but also lots of publisher-specific news. As a trade weekly, it's expensive, but your local library probably has a subscription.

- **Books in Print.** This multi-volume directory is available at all libraries. With it, you can search for books by subject (among other ways)—a quick way to survey not only what's forthcoming, but what has already been published on a given subject.

- *The Internet.* Finally, you have some great book-research tools on the Information Superhighway. The Internet is filled with book reviews and discussion sites. And there are the online booksellers. They offer quick access to information on specific titles and authors. And the best provide very interesting cross-references to similar books. You can research books that might compete with one you're writing. Sometimes, you can see what other titles readers of a given title are buying. And the sales-rank feature found at most booksellers' sites tells you what's selling best. No matter what, you can almost always take high sales as indicative of what publishers want. See Appendix A for the URLs of major online booksellers.

Writer's Magazines and Market Books

Finally, essential market information is found in two books, *The Writer's Handbook* and *Writer's Market*. Each has its strengths, and while there is a lot of overlap, each has enough listings that the other doesn't to make it worthwhile to have both books.

Then there are the market listings in the magazines: *The Writer*, *Writer's Digest*, and similar magazines. No particular magazine's listings are comprehensive or exclusive; they each provide an approach to what they consider to be solid, in-depth information, in the context of an interesting, wide-ranging selection. I always check more than one magazine to keep up with markets, and I recommend you do the same.

Another good source of market info for book proposals is the annual *Writer's Guide to Book Editors, Publishers, and Literary*

Agents, by Jeff Herman. The book is subtitled *Who They Are! What They Want! And How to Win Them Over!*

Those with specialized writing interests may find more specialized market books useful. Among these are *Children's Writer's & Illustrator's Market* (Writer's Digest Books), *The Christian Writers' Market Guide* (Harold Shaw Publishers), *Novel and Short Story Writer's Market* (Writer's Digest Books), *Poet's Market* (Writer's Digest Books), and *Writer's Online Marketplace* (Writer's Digest Books).

But remember: Printed information may be slightly dated. The market listings in the latest issue of a magazine were put together nearly three months before the cover date. The information in an annual book directory can be as much as a year out of date.

Always verify and expand on any such information before you act on it.

My First Encounters with Market Listings

I don't know the exact date, but I do happen to know the exact time of day that I started writing with intent to publish. It was a morning late in the summer of 1971, at 9:05 a.m.

How do I know? At the time, I worked the midnight shift in a Ford Motor Company transmission plant. That morning, I left the factory around 8:30 a.m. Driving home, I stopped at a mall, which had a Waldenbooks store. (Actually, it was "Walden Books" at the time. Smashed-word names hadn't come into fashion yet.)

The store opened at 9:00 a.m., and I was the first (and only) customer. Characteristically, I headed straight for the science fiction books. I scanned for new titles, but after the last shelf, I overscanned right into the reference section. One title jumped out at me.

It was *Writer's Market*. I remember thinking, "I wonder if that's what I think it is?"

I pulled the book from the shelf and looked through it. It was what I thought it was: a gold mine for a fledgling writer. And it listed magazines that I read regularly.

This book was a revelation. I bought it, and remember glancing at my watch, thinking I might get something to eat before I headed home to sleep. 9:05, the watch read. I dithered for about three seconds, then decided to head home straightaway so I could browse this new (to me) book.

For the next year, I read the seemingly endless market listings several times a week. I started writing and soon selling my work. Not surprisingly, my first sale to a national magazine, *Modern People*, came about because the description in *Writer's Market* convinced me that this magazine was just the right place for my wacky humor. I sent in a manuscript and got back a $25 check. I had made a sale!

When I thought I'd seen all the neat resources for writers, I found an intriguing book in a used bookstore. An odd-sized book it was, with an orange cover. It measured perhaps 4" by 7" and it was thick. I've always believed that odd-sized books are almost always interesting, so I pulled it from the shelf.

It turned out the book was *Writers' and Artists' Yearbook*, a market directory published in England, geared to the British freelancer. Still, it listed some American markets, and I felt I might benefit from a different viewpoint on those. And I found the listings for markets in Great Britain intriguing.

At that time, in 1975, writing for magazines in England seemed a novel way to get published, so I sent a manuscript off to a magazine called *Practical Householder*. The article sold, and a few weeks later I received a check (or cheque) in the amount of ten English pounds sterling. (That took a couple weeks to cash!)

I received a copy of the magazine soon after—plus a prize! The prize was a pewter "whistling tankard," awarded for the best article in that issue.

That sale encouraged me to submit more articles to British

markets. I continued sending the occasional article to Britain well into the 1980s. Some were offered as reprints, and some were original. Most paid at least a small amount.

The moral: Never stop looking for new market resources.

And don't be afraid to try something new.

One of the recurring themes in this book is selling more. But what if business fails to take off quickly, or slows down, in spite of everything you're doing?

The next chapter deals with that "what if." I'll show you a bit more about getting more writing work, looking for "outside work," and some bootstrapping activities you can do to expand your writing skills into related areas.

Putting Networking to Work

Finally, a few words on networking and marketing. Finding and developing opportunities to sell what you write is one of the primary goals of networking. Information gleaned from a casual Internet chat or a regular forum may offer news about a new editor, a new magazine, or a new book line.

For instance, in the late 1980s, the members of the Science Fiction Writers of America had a private message board on the Genie online service. I recall that Jane Yolen, award-winning author and editor of many short-story collections, often announced the theme of an upcoming anthology to that group, inviting anyone to submit appropriate work.

The group's Web site now serves the same purpose (in a "for members only" area). Other national writers' groups have similar areas for their members, where information exchange is the main activity (whether it's gossip, market news, or writing opportunities).

You can network similarly at open Web sites for writers. Participate in the message boards and share news of your own, as you look for useful info. Sooner or later you'll come across useful contacts and market leads. And as you become known as an experienced writer, someone may contact you privately about an opportunity.

Networking is a time-honored tradition in all professions. It is particularly important for writers, who mostly work alone. Because of that, attending a writers' workshop, a readers' convention (which always draws writers and often editors), or meeting another professional writer for a one-on-one chat makes quite a difference in one's enthusiasm for writing. Why? Because you get to "talk shop" with other writers who are doing what you are doing—with people who understand what it's really like.

Other writers can fill you in on who's buying what, who got fired or quit, got divorced or married, how much did so-and-so get for her new novel, what's he really like in person, and so on.

If you haven't been involved in gatherings of writers, get to one. If nothing else, it's fun! The informal element of gossip often offers the biggest and most surprising benefits.

How to Locate Writer Gatherings

Here are some ways to locate conferences, trade shows, and conventions where you can network with other writers.

- *Writers' conferences.* You will find an extensive listing of writers' conferences in every May issue of *Writer's Digest*, as well as in almost every issue of *The Writer*. Educator journals, such as the journals of the National Council of Teachers of English (NCTE, see its Web site at www.ncte.org) or the International Reading Association (IRA, www.ira.org) are another good source of events that feature many prominent and lesser-known writers. Also, professional associations of writers (see Appendix A for organizations for travel writers, journalists, and so on)—often have regular meetings and conferences, both national and regional.

- *Trade shows.* Check the Web sites and trade journals that cover the fields you're interested in for trade show announcements.

(For example, the BEA is announced in *Publishers Weekly*, and at the American Bookseller's Association Web site.)

- *Genre-fiction conventions.* For mystery writers' and fans' conventions, a good source is the Mystery Writers of America (MWA) Web site: http://www.mysterywriters.org/. For romance writers, try *Romantic Times* magazine. For science fiction and fantasy writers, watch for announcements in magazines such as *Analog* and *Isaac Asimov's Science Fiction Magazine*; also, *Locus* magazine maintains a good list at their Web site, www.locusmag.com.

As you will learn in the next chapter, these writer gatherings are also good places to meet agents and editors, who are important gate-keepers on your road to writing success.

CHAPTER 9

Relationships with Agents & Editors

OVER THE PAST 20 YEARS, the single most-frequently asked question I get from new writers is, "Do I need an agent?" Often, this is expressed presumptively as "How do I get an agent?" But is an agent indeed a necessity?

Over my career, I have worked at times with a couple of agents, but have ended up deciding to represent my work myself. The main reason, I think, is that I write in a diversity of areas; it is difficult to find an agent familiar with all of them.

And I find that I enjoy the marketing work. I like to get out and meet potential clients, and do a good job of maintaining relationships over time. Even when I am not working on a project for a given editor, I like to stay in touch, keeping the channels of communication open and always looking for new opportunities.

Still, you may need an agent. Let explain when and why. And what they can do for you, and what it will cost.

Do You Need an Agent?

There are instances when you need an agent. The most significant is dealing with the growing number of major book publishers that will not work with unagented writers.

Actually, some of those will work with an unagented writer; they just tell most people that they don't. As an oft-published writer, if I approach them on my own, they aren't going to tell me to "Get out of here—and don't come back without an agent!" They will gladly look at my proposal—and yours, if your credentials are compelling enough.

Still, the overwhelming majority will not work with unagented writers, no matter what. Michael Korda (former Editor-in-Chief of Simon & Schuster) makes a good case for writers using agents in his book *Another Life* (Random House, 1999). From Korda's perspective, dealing with an agent "is far more civilized than dealing with most authors." (But it's interesting to note that he has also dealt directly with many authors.)

From my own brief experience negotiating deals from the publisher's side of the desk, I can understand his statement. When talking about a deal with an agent, an editor doesn't have to explain all the ins and outs of the contract and its technicalities. An agent likely knows in rough terms your house's limit for new writers, experienced mid-list writers, and for bestselling writers. He or she knows how to play the game—what to shoot for, what's realistic, and when to vent his or her wrath over what he or she considers a "lowball" offer.

What Can an Agent Do for Me?

Depending on the agent, your work, and the editors to whom your work is submitted, here's what an agent often can do for you:

- Get your manuscript, sample chapters, or proposal to editors who are looking for the kind of writing you do. Since most agents know editors personally, and keep up with the day-to-day changes and developments that affect the work they represent, they are able to target the right market for your work. Unless you are really plugged into your portion of the publishing business, and know several editors personally, you may not be able to do any better.

- Get your manuscript noticed and read before those of writers who simply send theirs in cold, with no previous contact. This is especially true for agents who visit editors regularly—which is why many agents live in or near New York City, or travel there frequently.

- Get your book read at those publishing houses where the policy is "no unsolicited manuscripts." (You may be able to do the same yourself, but it's not easy.)

- Get you a better deal, financially. Some agents have "leverage." This may be in the form of big-name clients whose work editors want, a long business relationship or friendship with a given editor, or other connections. They may be able to use this leverage to get you a larger advance or a better royalty percentage or other beneficial contract terms. Or, based on their last eight deals with that publisher, they may know exactly how much beyond an initial offer an editor can go, and which contract points are negotiable. All contract offers can be improved—the question is how and how much.

When the Author Really Didn't Need an Agent

I recall negotiating one deal for a publisher who called to ask whether I could, on a freelance basis, help with direct negotiations with a very promising new author for a three-book contract. He went on to mention that she had an agent.

"Why don't you and the agent handle it?" I asked.

"Because I can't stand him!" was the reply. "I'll tell you about it another time, but I absolutely refuse to negotiate with that so-and-so."

So I called the writer, and offered the deal with the maximum advance the publisher would allow, and went over the royalties and other contract terms.

She accepted the deal, and that was that.

As it happened, the author was an almost overnight success, and soon moved on to a high-powered literary agency—one that was more successful in representing their authors' interests without offending publishers.

RELATIONSHIPS WITH AGENTS & EDITORS   157

- Help you take advantage of new developments, such as a book publisher starting a new line. If the agent sees editors daily, and/or stays up-to-date on publishing industry developments, he or she can advise clients of potential new directions for their work, based on insider knowledge.

- Evaluate and provide suggestions to improve your work. Not all agents do this, but some will read an entire manuscript and make suggestions for you to improve it. Those agents do it out of the desire to present the best possible work to editors.

- Sell subsidiary rights, such as book excerpts, foreign-language editions, and film or movie rights. Some agents don't do this directly, but instead have cooperative arrangements with other agents who specialize in these areas. (Some publishers retain their own specialists to negotiate sub-rights sales for their books, such as foreign language rights, in which case they will want to have a contract that allows them to pursue those options.)

- Find work for you. An agent who knows that a publisher or book packager is in need of certain types of books may be able to get a contract for you to write one of those books, or to ghost-write a book for a celebrity.

- Make sure advance and royalty payments are timely, with proper accounting. When you sign up with an agent, all of your money for the projects he or she represents goes through that agent. (The agent will take his or her percentage, then send you a check, with accounting.) It clearly behooves the agent to take whatever actions are necessary to ensure that a publisher's payment is on time.

An agent can also serve as a useful buffer between a publisher or editor and a writer. Where a writer may kill a deal by giving the editor a hard time over requested changes, or by making unreasonable demands ("Get me on Oprah's show, or I'm pulling the manuscript!"), a good agent knows how to play hardball, while keeping things on a friendly, professional level.

Finally, if you loathe or are afraid of having to deal with the fine-print quibbles of contract negotiations, you'll want to turn everything over to a good literary agent.

Agent Q&A

From talking with hundreds of writers and would-be writers, I know the questions that writers want answered about agents.

Q: Will an agent sell my articles and short stories?

A: Usually, no. Selling an article or short story is almost as much work as selling a book, but the money is likely a fraction of what placing a book brings in. Logically, agents would rather spend their time selling books. Some agents may handle the sale of shorter works for book clients as a favor, but mostly you'll have a difficult time finding an agent to handle articles, short stories, or poetry.

Q: How much does an agent get?

A: An agent receives a percentage of the amount you earn on sales of your work. This includes both the advance and any ensuing royalties on a book, no matter how many years the book pays

Your Marketing Platform

There is nothing in a nonfiction proposal more important than a marketing plan. Make suggestions for how the publisher can promote the book, and even more essential, tell the publisher how you can help. Do you have media contacts? Are you an experienced speaker? Do you have lists of newsletters in your field that might review or write about the book? Do you lecture at meetings where the book can be sold or flyers can be distributed? Do you have a Web site or belong to an organization that does and will promote your book? You get the idea. . . .

A marketing plan is not usually expected from a novelist, but it is a pleasant and welcome surprise if one is forthcoming. Fiction is promoted, too, by in-store placement, author appearances, book jacket blurbs. Sales of mysteries are helped by authors who are active in such organizations as the Mystery Writers of America (regional branches), Sisters in Crime, and other mystery writer organizations that support their members and boost their visibility. All novelists can start a minor groundswell by making themselves known at local bookstores, by placing items in neighborhood newspapers, and by using other local media. Some writers have reached out to store buyers with mailings of postcards, bookmarks, or reading copies.

Signal your readiness to participate, and make known what contacts you have, when you are approaching an agent.

—Nancy Love, agent, in "What Do Agents Want, in The Writer's Handbook 2002 royalties. This also includes subsidiary rights sales. For decades, the traditional cut used to be 10 percent. Nowadays it is 15 percent, although a good number of agents already have adopted or are considering an increase to 20 percent.

Some agents also charge clients for expenses such as postage, long-distance phone calls, and photocopying manuscripts. (I don't necessarily like paying out of my pocket for this, but it's a fairly common practice.)

Q: Can I get an agent before I have sold a book?

A: Maybe. New agents, and those who are expanding their client lists, are willing to take on newcomers. But only if the new writer's work is promising. And your work will probably not receive priority attention; agents will give more effort to manuscripts that are most likely to sell first—usually the work of more established writers.

Q: How much should I pay an agent?

A: Nothing! Zero, zip, zilch! Agents earn a percentage of any deal they make. At most, you may be charged for some expenses, as described a few paragraphs back, but you never pay an agent a "fee" to represent you. Never.

If an agent has to charge clients to handle their work, it does not speak well of his or her ability to sell manuscripts.

Q: What about reading fees?

A: Most real agents don't charge reading fees. They make money—a percentage of their clients' income—only when they sell books.

So-called "agencies" that charge "reading fees" or offer to critique your work and "get it into shape" for money are usually not the sorts of operations you want to represent your work. Sometimes (but not always) fee-based agencies are outright scams, set up to take your money with no guarantee of representation.

If you want to have your work critiqued, pay a criticism service to do it—not an operation set up to trick you out of your money under false pretenses. At the very least, ask around among authors and editors you know, to see if you can find any indication that the agency is legit and really does sell book manuscripts for writers.

Remember: If you can't sell your book, and can't find a legitimate agent to take you on, maybe you need to improve it . . . or work on something else.

How to Get an Agent

There are several ways to go about getting an agent. The simplest is to send samples of your work—usually an outline of a book you are writing or have written, along with a complete chapter from the book—to agents for their consideration. You can find the names and addresses of agents willing to look at the work of new writers in several key resources: two of the best are *Literary Market Place*, and *The Writer's Guide to Book Editors, Publishers, and Literary Agents*, by Jeff Herman.

If you have a friend who is a good-selling writer with an agent, ask your friend if he or she will recommend you to that agent. Recommendations from current clients are a common means whereby agents get new clients. Just don't count on results; if the agent feels that he or she can't sell your work, your friendship with a good client isn't going to

Association of Authors' Representatives

The Association of Authors' Representatives (AAR) is a professional organization for agents who represent book authors (fiction or nonfiction) and playwrights. To be an active member, an agent must meet a set of professional standards and agree to an ethical code of conduct, which includes not charging fees for reading or to evaluate an author's work (except for charges for postage and photocopying).

In general, a reputable agent:

- Does not charge a reading fee
- Does not charge a commission of more than 20 percent on domestic sales
- Is willing to disclose his/her career history, education, and credentials
- Sells and markets books or plays on a regular basis
- Does not own or have a financial interest in either an editing service or a subsidy publisher
- Does not refer an author to an outside service for which he/she would have to pay

A good place to begin your search is to check out the AAR's Web site at www.aar-online.org, which provides a list of agents who are members and who uphold the organization's professional standards.

make any difference. It's just a way to get your foot in the door; if your work isn't good enough, you'll find yourself right back outside that door very quickly.

No matter how you go about seeking an agent, you can market your book yourself to publishers in the meantime. And if you do get an offer for a book deal on your own, you might ask the editor for the name of a reputable agent—bearing in mind that some editors really dislike working with the most aggressive agents, because they cost the editors more money.

A final bit of advice: Study the book *How to Be Your Own Literary Agent: The Business of Getting a Book Published*, by Richard Curtis (Houghton Mifflin). Curtis, a literary agent for more than 30 years and author of a number of books himself, offers solid advice on how to be an informed author if you choose to work directly with publishers and editors. If you manage to find a literary agent, this book will help you understand and oversee what your agent is doing for you.

This excellent book will help you market your own work yourself. It explains a lot about book contracts and how the publishing business works.

Connecting with Editors

As self-evident as it is, it is worth mentioning that writers with good professional contacts tend to sell more (and often get better deals) than writers lacking such contacts.

Some writers don't like to hear that. I didn't—until I gained a few professional contacts myself, a couple years after my work was first published in a national magazine. It's just the way things work. When in Rome, do as the Romans do. (Or, as Robert A. Heinlein wrote, "If the natives rub blue mud in their bellybuttons, I rub blue mud in mine.")

No, you won't automatically sell everything you submit simply because you have good contacts. An example is my friend Betsy Mitchell. Back in the early 1980s, she was assistant editor of a magazine where I sold several stories. Later, she worked for the publisher of some of my novels, and ended up as an associate publisher with two of the biggest paperback publishing houses. But even though she likes my work, I wasn't able to sell a novel to her at her current position. She knows the specific needs of that publishing house, and like most editors, that's what drives her acquisitions decisions.

Despite friendships and professional acquaintances, you won't be able to sneak through anything that an editor wouldn't buy from someone else. But you may be able to get it looked at more closely. And a network of contacts can bring in work unexpectedly. An editor at Publisher A knows an editor at Publisher B who is looking for someone to write a book on three-prong blivets. The first editor remembers that you once worked at the factory where 95 percent of the three-prong blivets are made. She calls Editor B to refer him to you. After which, Editor B owes Editor A lunch, or a similar favor.

If you're connected, you often receive tips and information about who is looking for what. Such information might come from editors, publishers, agents, or other writers. I've been invited to contribute to original anthologies, among other things, because a fellow writer thought I would be a good person to include.

I've also been on the other end of this, recommending authors I knew to editors looking for good work. An editor at John Wiley & Sons (who had recently published two of my books) called to ask whether I could write a book about the Internet. This was in the early 1990s, when the Net and the Web and even online services were known to a vast minority of perhaps three million people.

But at the time, I had a book to finish, and one on the horizon. I told the editor that I couldn't—but knew someone who could: a technology writer named Paul Gilster. In his computer columns, Paul had been giving my books good reviews. I had contacted Paul to thank him for the good press (and incidentally, let him know what I was working on to be released soon). And we stayed in touch.

So I telephoned Paul, who wasn't sure he could write a book. But I knew that he could. It took a bit to convince him of that, but he finally agreed to contact the editor. Paul signed the contract and wrote one of the first and best books about the Internet (*The New Internet Navigator*, Wiley). He's been going strong ever since.

If nothing else, knowing an editor means that your manuscripts will get into the "read first" pile. And other benefits may come your way. An editor friend once referred me to someone looking for a speaker for a writers' conference (to replace another writer who had backed out). I was paid very nicely for about five hours of lectures, plus a week's expense-paid vacation in St. Petersburg, Florida, in January. (If you live in Ohio, as I do, you can understand why I was thrilled; Ohio winters are cold!) And I was invited back the year following, too.

How to Meet Editors

Most freelancers work by mail, e-mail, and telephone, and never meet their editors. However, more than a few would benefit from the opportunity to actually meet editors to present ideas and manuscripts—and to get to know them better as people and professional colleagues.

When you present your work to an editor in person, you have the editor's immediate and undivided attention. Your work is certain to get some extra attention not only then but also in the future; the editor will remember you as a person when he or she reviews your submissions.

I'm assuming, of course, that you're neither obnoxious nor a complete twit. Meeting editors in person can be unproductive, unless you present yourself as the kind of professional with whom they will want to work. That's why I'll offer some ground rules for meeting editors on their home turf.

Meeting Editors on Their Turf

The basic rules for such meetings are simple:

- Make sure you're expected. Don't just "drop in," unannounced. Contact the editor or agent you wish to meet by mail, e-mail, or phone first, and set up a specific date and time for a meeting. The venue might be the editor's office, or it might be a lunch or dinner meeting. Ask the editor what his or her preference is for the venue. (And it's accepted practice that whoever does the inviting for lunch or dinner is also the one who pays.)

- Don't meet without a purpose. You'll waste the editor's time (and yours) if you drop by just to see if there's anything the editor has on his or her mind. Instead, propose that you meet to discuss your own specific project or projects (manuscript, outline, or proposal). Establish exactly what you intend to present when you set up the meeting. And bring the materials, well-organized and ready to view, with clean, crisp copies to leave with the editor.

- Conduct yourself in a businesslike, yet informal, manner. You don't have to approach the meeting as if you're addressing a corporate board meeting, but you shouldn't go in acting as if you and the editor are long-lost friends, either.

- Don't oversell yourself or your work. Telling an editor you are a great writer, or that your book will "sell a million copies" will give the editor the impression that you are naïve or unrealistic.

- Don't wear out your welcome. When it's time for the meeting (or lunch or dinner) to end, say farewell and thanks. (The editor will either have set a time limit for the meeting, or will give you some obvious cues when you've exhausted the topic and/or he must turn to other matters.)

As you can see, the rules for meeting an editor (or an agent) are like those for any other kind of business meeting. Set a time, venue, and purpose for the meeting, conduct yourself in a proper manner, and don't be pushy. Offer specific ideas or materials, but also listen carefully and inquire if there are other needs the editor might have and want to share.

Meeting Editors at Events

It is also possible to meet editors outside of their or your normal habitat. Magazine and book editors frequently speak at writers' conferences sponsored by colleges and writers' organizations around the country.

They also attend conventions in their areas of interest. These include gatherings of genre-fiction readers and writers (science fiction and fantasy, mystery, horror, and romance). There are also book-trade conventions, such as the annual Book Expo America (BEA) and the computer industry's COMDEX trade shows. Most publishers send staff to manage sales booths, and the retinue often includes editors.

Besides the large national events, there are many regional events. You can probably find several writers' conferences, genre fiction conventions, or industry trade shows within a couple hours' drive from your home.

You can meet editors informally during the receptions and parties that always accompany such functions. However, you can conduct little, if any, business at these social affairs, and a lot of other writers, some better known than you, are likely to be chatting with editors and agents for the same reasons as you.

The best you can hope for when you meet an editor or agent casually—at the booth, banquet, or table, or wandering the floor—is to make a good first impression, hoping to be remembered by that person when your work later crosses his or her desk. Be prepared to hand out a card, and suggest that you might call someday soon to discuss an idea you have for a submission.

But avoid talking about it in any more detail. A casual encounter is not the best time to make a lengthy presentation. Trying to do so will just make the editor squirm; he or she probably has other things to do at that moment. Just say how pleased you are to meet them (this suggest you think they do good work), and let them move on gracefully.

Don't be pushy. To make a good impression at informal meetings, there is one cardinal rule: Don't force your writing into the conversation. Doing so gives the editor the idea that the only thing you're interested in is pushing your work—just like 9,000 other writers. If the editor asks you about your writing, fine. Otherwise, concentrate on making a good impression. Most editors feel it's somewhat tasteless and rude to press business details on someone in such an informal situation.

Plan Meetings in Advance

But if it's not appropriate to discuss my writing at an informal meeting, when can I? It's easy: Set up a private meeting, in advance. A few writers' conferences block out time and set up such meetings with editors or agents for conference attendees (sometimes charging a fee). But if not, you'll have to make the arrangements yourself.

Write or phone the editor(s) or

When They Come to See You

Do editors really travel to meet writers?

In Another Life, Michael Korda talks about traveling often to meet writers, usually bestselling authors, of course. Not all of his meetings with writers were fun for him. (Harold Robbins, Jacqueline Susann, and Joan Crawford weren't.)

But Korda wasn't always visiting well-known authors. He spent a lot of time with Carlos Castaneda before (and after) Simon & Schuster published Castaneda's books. Editors sometimes even travel to meet lesser-known writers, sometimes because of personal interests, sometimes just because other travel plans bring them to the locale.

When editors come from New York to southwestern Ohio to meet me, we get little work done. We talk about books, mostly the Current Book, perhaps for a half-hour. One editor in particular, Burt Gabriel, my editor at Simon & Schuster's Brady imprint for seven or eight years, visited now and then. Burt was the nicest editor anyone could work with.

Whenever he came to Ohio, we would have dinner at a very famous and very old restaurant, The Golden Lamb.

I didn't give it much thought at the time, but Burt always showed up with his sons, who lived in Columbus, Ohio, with their mother.

It occurred to me years later that Burt probably found the trips a great way to visit his kids on his expense account. Way to go, Burt!

agent(s) you're trying to contact at least a month in advance of the conference or convention. If you wait till later, their schedules will likely be full. Explain who you are, and ask if it would be possible to meet for lunch (or dinner, breakfast, coffee, a drink, or whatever) during the conference. You'll find that many editors are open to such an invitation (especially with your implicit offer to buy).

Don't despair if for some reason you can't reach a particular editor or agent in advance. It is possible to find them at the conference, and ask to set up a meeting for the next day. (This is far more tasteful than trying to discuss your writing in a crowded room, during a party or reception or after a lecture.) If they are too booked, they will tell you so.

The same rules apply here as with a "home-turf" meeting. Set a definite time, have a definite project (or projects) to present, and don't be pushy or oversell yourself. In addition, observe these tenets:

- Do not bring along a manuscript expecting the editor or agent to read it then and there. Editors and agents are busy at a conference or convention or show, and guard their time jealously. And they expect to have a little bit of time off. My editor at Simon & Schuster summed up his editorial viewpoint on writers' conferences: "Despite the demand, we aren't on duty 24 hours a day."

- Don't expect an editor or agent to carry your manuscript back to his or her office. As Betsy Mitchell, Associate Publisher at Warner Books, noted, "Editors don't plan on taking a lot of extra luggage back with them from a convention or conference. If an editor's interested in your manuscript, you'll be asked to mail it in."

- The prominent writers who speak at conferences deserve the same consideration. Don't ask them to read your work, no matter how much you really want to. (Unless, of course, having your work read and critiqued is a part of the writers' conference program.) Every published author, from Andre Norton and Stephen King to Tom Clancy—even Michael Banks—is besieged with requests to read beginning writers' work, and we normally decline the honor for the same reason: We're too busy with our own work.

You may not make an immediate sale by following these guidelines, but you will open some doors. And that's the first step.

CHAPTER 10

Sources of Extra Income

THE TIME MAY COME WHEN you need to generate some extra income. Perhaps business and income have slowed down for whatever reasons, or perhaps you are just trying to bridge a slight gap until your next royalty check arrives.

Here are a few suggestions to help you find extra work. Some involve different kinds of writing (not necessarily for publication). Others don't involve writing per se, but make use of your specialized knowledge and skills.

As a freelance writer, you have more skills than just the ability to write. You know how to research topics and how to tailor your work to specific market interests. You know how to create, edit, sell, and deliver work on time. You know the basics of good bookkeeping, record-keeping, and project management.

Besides that, if you are making your living writing, you likely have a lot of knowledge on the topics that you write about that you can share with others, especially if they are willing to pay you for it. This chapter covers some of the best ways to share your knowledge and expertise for money in ways beyond writing for publication.

Teaching "Writing & Getting Published" Courses

I have taught occasional courses in writing for publication for a long time.

I do this for several reasons. First, the money is welcome. Second, the courses are an opportunity to get out of the house and interact with other people. Third, this serves as continuing education for me, as I consider how to teach the best techniques and methods of writing to aspiring writers.

There's one more thing I get out of teaching these courses: Inspiration. It's a real joy to interact with others eager to write, to discuss and think about literary structures, writing style and technique, marketing, and all the other elements of writing for publication.

What's Involved?

Most community-based education programs, whether public school districts, community recreation programs, technical colleges, or area universities, have what's called an Adult Education or Continuing Education program.

These programs have varied names, such as "Lifelong Learning" or "Communiversity." Most operate in pretty much the same way. Using the facilities of a university, school, or community building, they offer enrichment and how-to classes in writing, painting, computers, music, financial investing, and so on.

Here and there, you find courses offering certification in some profession. Some universities also offer credits for certain classes.

In some larger cities you may find commercial operations that run such programs for profit.

How Much Can You Earn?

The pay is usually pretty good. The practice for community-based programs with which I'm familiar is to pay the class instructor one-third to one-half of the students' fees (or, as I like to say, "the gate"). The last check I received for doing a three-week course (one two-hour session per week) was over $700. Not bad for six hours in class, plus about the same in preparation and reviewing student papers. That works out to $65 per hour, in 2002 dollars. Not bad!

The commercial operations tend to offer hourly wages that aren't as great—perhaps $15 to $20 per hour—but good enough to attract some people to teach, especially when you consider the positive side benefits of teaching.

Breaking In

To get started as a teacher of continuing education classes, you need:

- Willingness and time (including for travel and class preparation, besides class time).

- An outline or syllabus. This should present the topics you intend to cover in each session and the overall goals of your class. Also, list books you will require students to read (if any), and any supplies needed.

Critiquing Manuscripts

As a professional writer and teacher, you may get people approaching you with requests to edit or critique their manuscripts for a fee.

If you agree to do this, be aware that it can be very time-consuming. Oddly, you'll discover that the better writers may require more of your time than average or sub-par writers. This is because when their work has problems with style, technique, or other elements, it tends to be subtle and may take longer to figure out.

And if the writer wants to discuss the fine points, you're committed to even more time.

I once took on the task of editing a whole novel independently for a writer. I got paid in advance; still, it was not worth the money. The fee seemed good at first, but I spent more time on the project than anticipated, which took me away from my own writing.

Other problems may emerge. You could end up being blamed for the writer's manuscript not selling. (This didn't happen to me, but it's happened to other friends who took on such work.)

Before undertaking any work, prepare an agreement to be signed by you and your client. This should state exactly what you will do—how detailed the level of your edit or critique will be.

And make it clear in writing that you in no way guarantee a sale or anything else beyond the professional services rendered.

- A proposal of the time and length of each session, how many sessions, and the ideal dates to meet. You can base this on the target program's typical offerings, such as 7 to 9 p.m., Tuesdays, for six weeks.

- A brief resume or c.v. (curriculum vitae) of your writing credits and credentials.

Then, start making contacts. Request current brochures from existing programs in your area. Telephone school districts or universities in your area to ask if they sponsor a continuing education program. If so, would they be interested in the course you want to offer? You can propose topics that are broad ("Writing and Getting Published"), or specialized ("Writing Your Novel").

There are two things to keep in mind when you start a class. First, just about every unpublished writer wants a professional writer to read and comment on his or her work. Allow for this in planning your course. How you choose to handle it is up to you. You can ask students to rewrite a few paragraphs they enjoyed reading from another work, or have them prepare a description of and sample from one of their own writing projects. You might agree to look at entire manuscripts, but if you do, be prepared to spend more time than you ever expected.

It's better to limit this right from the beginning by defining exactly how much of each student's work you will read and critique. Your students have paid to tap into your knowledge.

Make sure that you are presenting what students need to know, and present it in a positive way that is not unduly negative or damaging to sometimes fragile egos.

Speaking at Writers' Conferences

Being a speaker at a writers' conference usually pays well, and the work is mostly fun. In fact, I enjoy this so much that I once prodded a large writers' group in Cincinnati to put on a conference. It came off very well, and I got to give another talk!

Regional writers' clubs, universities, and other organizations sponsor writers' conferences all around the U.S. and in Canada. The typical setting is a university campus or a small conference center, with out-of-town attendees and speakers staying onsite or at a designated hotel. The two- to five-day event is normally a multi-track affair, with two or more speakers conducting sessions at the same time (in different rooms, of course).

A conference may or may not have a theme (fiction, books, women writers, and so on).

Most writing magazines carry a number of ads for upcoming writers' conferences, and often run more complete lists periodically throughout the year.

What's Involved?

As a guest speaker or instructor at a writers' conference you will be asked to conduct a certain number of sessions, perhaps one per day during the conference. These might range from a four-hour seminar one day, to just an hour's talk or a panel discussion the next.

You may also be expected to attend an opening ceremony or banquet at the beginning, and perhaps a similar event at the end.

In between scheduled sessions, you should plan to make yourself available for informal discussions with attendees. It's a nice touch, and much appreciated by all. You will always find it invigorating to talk with all the serious new writers, and being friendly, positive, accessible, and full of good advice will make it more likely you will get asked back in a coming year.

How Much Can You Earn?

You normally get a flat fee, plus expenses (airfare or other transportation costs, hotel, and meals). The amount varies, but generally the honorarium is enough to make the gig worthwhile. I've made as little as $550 for speaking six times over three days, and from $500 to $850 for speaking once or twice in one day.

Also, a local bookstore or conference book vendor may order your books to sell before and during the event. Sometimes, speakers are encouraged to bring their own copies of their titles to sell in the back of the room after their sessions, always a nice source of extra compensation.

You also get to meet other writers of note. I recall especially a wonderful experience being in a writer-in-residence program with the late John Ciardi. Many conferences also have influential editors and agents on their programs. Overall, it's a good opportunity to talk shop and network extensively.

I've also been able to visit friends and relatives in distant cities, with someone else paying the travel expense.

Getting Started

Usually the invitation to speak at a writers' conference comes out of the blue—from someone who has read your articles on writing, or otherwise knows of your credits.

The one conference to which I invited myself came from writing a letter offering my services (modestly) and my credentials. You can do the same. Otherwise, it's a matter of waiting until someone notices you. But keeping your name and work visible in writer networks regionally or nationally never hurts.

Reviewing Book Manuscripts

As you may know, nonfiction book editors sometimes use expert reviewers to evaluate proposals and completed book manuscripts. Expert reviewers are particularly important to publishers when professional, technical, or reference subjects are involved. The majority of such reviewers are freelance writers, who happen to have personal knowledge or expertise appropriate to a given book project.

Whether your expertise is based on a professional or avocational background is usually immaterial, as long as you have expert-level knowledge of the subject. (However, books in such highly technical fields as medicine and chemistry require review by peer professionals.)

Over the past ten years, I've reviewed dozens of manuscripts and proposals on such diverse topics as computer applications, writing, remote sensing devices, and the Soviet manned space program. This has generated some nice checks, and improved my knowledge of what editors like to see. I've also learned to watch for certain common mistakes in my own work—mistakes I might never have spotted, had I not seen them in other writers' manuscripts.

Fiction editors often use synopses and brief critiques of unsolicited submissions to help decide whether a manuscript is worth considering more closely. This is a vital service, considering the number of unsolicited manuscripts most publishing houses receive. The requirements are familiarity with a specific genre, and a literary taste that editors trust. Usually this work is done by junior editorial assistants. Use of outside readers is scarce, and these assignments are more difficult for the writer to get than evaluating nonfiction.

What's Involved?

The work is fairly straightforward. You read the manuscript or proposal, write a report on it, and perhaps flag sections or passages in the manuscript that need revision or other attention. Writing the report is a lot like writing a book review—except that you are expected not only to cite the book's strengths and weaknesses, but also to correct factual errors and provide specific input to make the manuscript a better book.

How Much Can You Earn?

The editor who offers this work to you will offer a flat rate for the job. The money's not bad for nonfiction—typical fees may range from $250 to $500. (I was once offered $1,800 to review a hefty computer book manuscript. This, for spending eight to ten hours with a 400-page manuscript.) Manuscript evaluation jobs can lead to other things, too—like selling your own book, or freelance editing assignments.

Some editors provide reviewer guidelines; some don't. All with whom I've worked require that you maintain both a writer's and a reader's viewpoint, and that you don't get personal in your critique.

For novels, there is not a lot of work available; the pay is low and it's harder to break in, unless you have a personal contact with a fiction editor.

Breaking In

To get started as a nonfiction reviewer, prepare a brief resume describing your area of expertise. Include any related publishing credits. (Note: you don't have to confine yourself to just one area of expertise.)

Send your resume, or c.v., along with a brief cover letter offering your services, to specific editors at various publishing houses who handle books on the subject(s) in which you have expertise. It's very important that you get the name of the editor in question; most editors are too busy to re-route a "cold-call" letter of this type.

To find the appropriate editor at a particular publishing house, check *Literary Market Place*. You might also telephone the publisher in question and ask for the name of the editor who handles your subject.

Personal networking can be useful, too. If you've sold a book, or have an encouraging conversation with an editor regarding a submission, let him or her know that you're available for manuscript and proposal evaluations. And if you have friends who have sold books, ask them to pass on your qualifications to their editors.

Freelance Editing

I have done some editing work over the years, especially on assembling some short-story anthologies. For a while in the 1980s, I was an Editorial Associate for a "book-azine" titled *New Destinies*, published by Baen Books. I screened story submissions, recommending some for publication (the final decision was made at higher levels). That was fun, as I got to read lots of very good science fiction stories.

I also got to read some very bad science fiction. Usually, I could tell the story was bad from the first page. Some of the writing was horrid; often the opening paragraph indicated that this was not a story anyone would buy. These easy-to-reject stories constituted more than 90 percent of all submissions. This also made me feel very good about my own writing.

What's Involved?

You will note that my "editing" involved selecting and sometimes helping shape material to be published. I did no hands-on manuscript editing. Mostly what I did was

How I Got Into Manuscript Reviewing

The first I heard of manuscript reviewing (outside of academic publishing) was about 15 years ago, when one of my own book manuscripts was sent out to an expert reviewer.

I was idle at the moment, so I asked my editor about the prospects of getting this work myself, and he said he would keep me in mind for any technical reviews. I thought about it a bit, and called several publishing houses to see whether they used expert or technical reviewers.

The first three didn't. I called the fourth (McGraw-Hill) to learn that the editor I was trying to reach had just left the company. As it happened, the new editor needed a partial manuscript reviewed immediately.

I happened to know enough about the subject to qualify. I read and reported on two chapters, an outline, and the proposal—and picked up $450 for my time.

read a lot of material as quickly as possible, and made recommendations on the good stuff.

Hands-on editing is more likely to be a full-time job. Those freelancers who do receive such freelance editing assignments tend to be former editors who have stayed in contact with the publishing houses where they worked.

How Much Can You Earn?

Freelance editing services usually bill on an hourly basis, though some fast editors work on a flat-rate basis. How much you bill (and if you are compensated for any expenses) depends on the publisher, the material, and you.

It has been my experience that editing is something writers should do only if they have nothing else to do. In my experience, the pay tends to be on the lower end of "average."

Breaking In

To get into freelance editing, it helps to know an editor or publisher personally, someone who knows you and your capabilities.

Often, it's a matter of being in the right place at the right time. If you're available and held in esteem by editors, sooner or later someone will offer you work. Or you will hear about some work you can do, and propose that you do it.

Some writing professionals enjoy this kind of work enough to set themselves up as a freelance editing bureau, offering a full range of services from early critiques of manuscripts to detailed copy-editing and proofreading. But beware: This work is time-consuming. Too much of it will definitely interfere with the time to write your own work.

Consulting as an Expert in Your Field

Are you an expert in something? If you have written a book in a given field, chances are you can turn your knowledge (and book contents) into a lecture, a training course, or a consulting role. Once you write a book about something, people assume you are an expert on the subject. (Hopefully, you are.)

Beginning in 1997, I wrote several books about Internet crime, about strange people on the Net, and other related subjects.

Thanks to two of those books, I was invited to join an international organization called the High Tech Crime Investigators Association (HTCIA). Under the auspices of the HTCIA, I have given talks to police, parole officers, FBI, and U.S. Customs agents. The talks paid well and researching them and meeting professionals in the field further increased my knowledge of online crime (providing fodder for articles and future books).

I've also consulted on the use of computers in law-enforcement applications, and helped track down some perpetrators. Some of that work followed the publication and national publicity (I was on the *Sally Jesse Raphael Show* and many radio shows as an expert) for another book of mine, *Web Psychos, Stalkers, and Pranksters.*

In addition to getting paid, such talks obviously help promote continued sales of your book(s).

What's Involved?

The range of activities in which you can be involved includes lecturing, demonstrations, consulting, and training in your subject area.

As you might imagine, you must be comfortable speaking to large groups of people. The more outgoing, entertaining, and well-prepared you are, the better. Beyond that, the work involves some extra writing to create professional-looking hand-outs, and some travel.

How Much Can You Earn?

The potential for cashing in on your publishing credits and related knowledge is unlimited. You may be invited to give a speech at a major event for a $1,000 fee. Or you might get $40 or $60 or more per hour as a consultant.

The pay varies; it depends on how interested the market is in your knowledge, and your credits, contacts, and charisma.

Breaking In

Sometimes opportunities find you, but usually, you have to sell yourself. The more you've published about your subject area, the easier it is to do this successfully.

How do you sell your knowledge? Search among professional organizations, manufacturers, publishers, and social groups. Any sort of organization that has meetings is a candidate for your services. The annual meetings of corporations, for instance, as well as "retreats" to which manufacturers and publishers send their employees, are potential venues. Even trade shows and government organizations can be a market.

Anyone who has a product falling within your subject area—including manufacturers and publishers—is a potential market for your consulting or promotional skills.

Whatever the venue, if participants can go away from your sessions with practical knowledge or developed skills, you will find an audience.

Many such markets can be approached by writing a letter to the key person in a given department, offering your services. You should be very precise about what you have to offer. Include a summary of your credentials and, if possible, a copy of your book.

Personal contacts are often a better means of finding a

market. Also, there are speakers' agencies around the country who book expert speakers. (Check the listings for speakers' agents in *Literary Market Place*.)

Other Writing Venues

There are other ways to make money writing, without publication or public credit. You won't get on anyone's bestseller list with these activities. Nor will your friends and relatives be able to pick up copies of a book or magazine to read your work therein. However, you will be paid—often very generously.

Writing for Ad Agencies & PR Firms

Working for advertising agencies and public-relations firms can be an excellent avenue to explore when you're looking for writing jobs.

What's Involved?

Advertising and PR clients need all sorts of writing. Here are just a few examples:

- Advertisements for print, radio, TV, and Internet outlets (writing complete scripts or simply ad copy)

- Speeches (for high-ranking corporate or organization executives, and for politicians)

- Newsletters and magazines for nonprofit organizations and companies

The ad and PR people often operate on very tight deadlines (sometimes they have to produce something for a client literally overnight). Accordingly, their need for freelance services waxes and wanes, depending on current projects and schedules.

How Much Can You Earn?

You may be paid by the job, or the hour. Most ad and PR agencies have fairly fixed ideas of what they are willing to pay. If you are asked, quote high, but indicate that your rates are flexible. They are looking for good, confident writers, not cheap ones. A respectably professional rate, plus good examples of past work, will earn you respect and some assignments.

Getting Started

If you know someone at an agency, let them know you are available, and provide samples of your work.

Otherwise, put together a package with some samples of your published work, a listing of your best credits, and a resume-like list of related skills and knowledge in areas besides writing. Send this—with a one-page cover letter expressing your desire to work with the agency on a freelance basis—to the agency's creative director. Then wait.

Writing for Businesses & Nonprofit Organizations

Large companies and nonprofit organizations offer a wealth of opportunities. You can often get work direct from them (taking a shortcut around the agencies). You can write articles for company publications (in-house or for the public), interpretations of technical matters for management, and company histories.

For instance, on several occasions I've written instruction manuals for consumer products; these proved to be among the best-paying jobs I've ever had.

I've also written for small businesses. The first time I did this, a new printer had just opened in my town. I needed some printing done, so I offered to trade my writing for his printing. He liked the idea. It saved him time—and I was a better writer than he was.

I ended up writing three different letters to solicit business. One letter was written to send to a general mailing list, another to local businesses, and a third solicitation letter was targeted for brides-to-be.

At one time or another I've written newsletters for churches and for a Red Cross chapter, and polished resumes and grant proposals.

How Much Can You Earn?

When it comes to businesses, organizations, and individuals, the pay rates vary widely. Here are a few real-life examples of my own earnings:

- $21,400 for writing and producing two 40-page manuals for a consumer product for a large company. (I netted $9,000, after subcontracting a printing company to do layout and paste-up.)

- $6,000 for writing one 50-page manual for a different product (no typesetting or layout involved).

- $45 per hour for writing a military technical training manual.

- $450 for a 2,000-word article for an in-house magazine of a large multi-national corporation.

Clearly, there is money to be made by offering your services to businesses that need and are willing to pay for good, clear writing.

The Best-Selling Author of . . . Sales Meetings?

Back in the 1970s, on several occasions I had a chance to discuss the writing life with John Jakes (author of North and South, and many other bestselling historical novels).

Jakes lived in Dayton, Ohio, and often dropped in to visit the occasional literary salon hosted by a UD professor for science fiction fans in the area. (Jakes had also written several science fiction novels in the early 1960s.)

At one gathering, Jakes mentioned to me that, before becoming a bestselling author, he had made a living by "writing sales meetings"— designs, outlines, and creative scripts for large corporate annual meetings. At first he had worked for an ad agency, then freelanced writing scripts for these meetings. He said the work was minimal, and the money good.

Apparently good enough to support him while he wrote some of his novels. Eventually, after winning a lawsuit involving the rights to his bestsellers, and with a film made from North and South, John Jakes relocated to one of the exclusive island communities off the coast of Georgia, where he still writes.

Breaking In

Like advertising and PR writing, it helps to know someone at the company for which you wish to do freelance work. I have had nice freelance writing jobs with the world's largest manufacturer of consumer household products, and one of the "Big Three" automakers. To get one of these, I replied to a classified ad in the local newspaper, but for the others, I knew someone in the department responsible for assigning the work.

To seek work, send a letter and samples of your work to the appropriate person in a corporate department or nonprofit organization's management. The trick is determining who is the right person—and when and why a company needs what kind of writing done. (A quick tip: Corporations are big on anniversaries—25th, 50th, 100th, and so forth. But remember: They start planning one to three years before that anniversary year.)

Dealing with small businesses is easier. You can simply walk in and chat with the owner. You don't have to make a pitch the first time you have a conversation. In each case where I did writing for small businesses, I took time first to establish a relationship, sometimes as a customer. I eventually brought up the subject in conversation, wondering what sort of promotion or advertising the owner did. That's when the sales pitch started.

Combining Writing with a Part-Time Job

On occasion, a freelance writer can experience a drastic drop in income. In a pinch, the fastest and most obvious way to bring in extra cash is to take a part-time job.

A part-time job doesn't have to be a disaster. With the right schedule, such a job may not even interfere with your writing very much. Actually, you may find that you enjoy getting out for a few hours each day and interacting with people. You'll certainly enjoy the extra cash and security.

What sort of job should a writer take? One that suits the

writer. The job may involve skills related to your old full-time job. For example, if you were in air-conditioning installation and repair before you went full-time as a writer, you can certainly find a few hours' work in this line every week. The same is true if you were formerly a computer programmer, appliance salesperson, or accountant.

You may find it more appealing to follow your hobby or personal interests. If you are into classic cars, you might enjoy taking a temporary part-time job in an auto parts store, as I did. Or, if you do a lot of home improvement, working in a hardware store could be your thing.

Whatever the job, and whatever your motivation in choosing it, always keep in mind that the position is temporary. Your real job is writing; the part-time work is simply a means of bringing in cash. It isn't forever.

But if you are gregarious, getting out and interacting with people isn't such a bad thing for a writer. You may stumble into some interesting topics—or characters—to write about. I know I did. And the short break from writing was refreshing. After my stint behind the counter serving customers, I found myself eager to return each day to my writing projects.

CHAPTER 11

On Persistence

IF YOU ARE LIKE ME—and many other writers—when on the verge of embarking on a freelance career, you have been thinking a lot about what you would do if you were to wash out as a full-time writer.

What will you do if you can't hack it? The simple answer is, "Get a job." But in this chapter you'll learn that there are many options for the full-time writer who is forced to return to the work force.

The options include going back your old job with gusto, or finding a different job in the same field. Perhaps you might prefer changing fields entirely. Or how about taking a job as a salaried writer? Or creating a job based on your writing expertise?

You could even begin to lay the groundwork for a second shot at writing freelance for a living. It's been done.

It's Your Life to Live

I strongly support anyone who tries to do something more with their life—those who seek fulfillment beyond work and family

On Success

The only place success comes before work is in the dictionary.

—Vince Lombardi

and hobbies. Those who go back to school after age 40, who decide to become full-time artists or writers—all have my admiration.

However, you must prepare properly before you take the plunge into writing for a living. It is important to strive to meet the criteria for being a full-time freelancer set forth in this book. Otherwise, you will not be fully prepared and may lose more than you gain. Worst of all, you may lose your dream.

If you're still on the road to writing full-time, good for you! However, if the realities presented in this book have discouraged you—that's a good thing, too. As the quote goes, "Anyone who can be dissuaded from writing, probably should be dissuaded."

In other words, if you do not think you can take on the challenges and pressure full-time writing involves, it is probably not for you.

Accept Responsibility for the Outcome

There is a final criterion to consider. This is to be able to accept everything that comes with the decision to become a full-time writer. That goes for the negative as well as the positive things we've discussed in this book.

If it happens that you don't make it as a full-timer, accept it and move on as gracefully as possible to the next phase of your life. Don't blame failure on your spouse or partner for not supporting you, or on the editors who've rejected your work, and certainly not on readers who didn't choose to buy your book or read your articles.

In the end, it is your actions, thoughts, and feelings that are responsible for your failures and successes. In short, *you* are responsible.

Still, accepting responsibility doesn't necessarily mean that you didn't do your personal best. Many things over which you have no power can leave your writing career in shambles. Still, selecting the full-time route is a choice you need to understand.

Accept the destination, and enjoy the sense of adventure travel—whether or not that road leads to success.

Why do I emphasize this? Because those who are unafraid to risk failure are affected less by its occasional dangers and setbacks. And they succeed more often.

So be bold. Learn to love the journey. And accept the ability to fail now and then. Many people—successful writers included—have in fact failed many times. So be prepared, and act responsibly.

Assessing Your Situation

Say it's July of 2010. You've been writing full-time for four years. You have a monthly magazine column, three books in print (and two out of print), and manage to sell a couple of articles to high-paying magazines every month. All this writing activity generated an income of just over $5,000 per month last year.

But one of the magazines goes out of business in August. At the end of September, you find that only one of your three books is paying royalties—and most of that eaten up by returns.

Suddenly, it looks as if your income is taking a nosedive. Your earnings dip to $3,500 per month.

Can it get worse? Yes—and it does!

In October, you learn that your column is axed because the publisher ordered the editors to cut expenses. Your column goes because your topic does not attract enough advertising.

Now you will be lucky to pull in more than $1,200 per month. That's just $14,400 per year. The only way you'll survive as a writer is if you're supported by a partner who loves you enough to be your patron. Or you have an exceptionally frugal lifestyle.

What should you do? Is it time to reconsider the career choice you've made?

Are You Doing the Right Things?

Do you quit? The answer lies in how you got into this situation.

Did you just realize it would have been a great idea to spread your work around, rather than cultivating just two magazines? And maybe you should have lined up a writing sideline (see Chapter 10), just in case your column got canceled?

In July, why weren't you finishing writing a new book under contract—while working on selling another one? You need to replace older books that have gradually declining royalties by looking to bring in cash advances for new ones.

If you let yourself become this vulnerable, yes—perhaps you should quit.

Or perhaps you can salvage your career if you learn very quickly from your mistakes. Always work to develop new markets so you never again find yourself in a similar desperate situation. Learn from the voice of experience—in this case, my experience. Yes, that scenario above is one that happened to me.

Accept from the beginning of your career that you must always have a backup plan in the works for every aspect of your writing business income. If you write a column or sell regularly to a few magazines, stockpile lists of article ideas that you can write and sell quickly to other kinds of magazines if some of your markets dry up. Better still, write and submit one of those alternative pieces to a magazine new to you. Even if it's rejected, you at least have established a contact.

Even if you write novels that sell well, consider outlining a nonfiction book or a novel of a different sort to keep on the back burner. You might even write a chapter now and then.

Finally, seek out some different kinds of writing work now and then, as discussed in Chapter 10. It's easier to turn to that sort of work in an emergency if you've been doing it occasionally—even if only once or twice a year.

"Winners Know When to Quit"

The old aphorism, "Quitters never win, and winners never quit" is a bit out of date, in my book. Sometimes quitting is winning. It takes a lot of guts to back off from something you really want to do. (This is doubly true if you've had to take a lot of criticism over it.)

But you aren't always quitting permanently when you make the choice to give up full-time writing to return to a salaried job. You can always work your way back to writing full-time.

The difficult part about making a major life-change is wondering whether your decision may be a mistake. You can agonize over this, but you may never really know. This being the case, be sure you are not quitting out of panic. Are you overlooking an income source? Are there other avenues to explore?

Henry Ford had a relevant motto. Ford, by the way, failed as an auto manufacturer several times before getting the right people behind him. He was also a book and newspaper publisher.

Ford was obviously a persistent sort—just as successful writers must be. Hence, here is his motto for your consideration:

"It's always too soon to quit."

If you find yourself at the crossroads, ask yourself if it is really too soon to quit. Do you have unexplored options? Is there another way to continue writing full-time?

Or are you deluding yourself and falling prey to wishful thinking?

What to Track: A Rule of Thumb

It's far easier to deal with a crisis and make a good decision if you see it coming in advance. Consider the difference between seeing the "Bridge Out" sign . . . and discovering the bridgeless chasm the hard way because someone stole the sign.

I suggest a simple rule of thumb. Keep track of the work and the money coming in every quarter. Calculate your average income per quarter. And at the end of each quarter—March, June, September, and December—take a look at what you've done over the past three months.

Then look three months ahead at what you've got lined up. If your income for the quarter just finished, or the next quarter ahead, drops to half or less of your average, it's time to take immediate action.

You don't have to panic, but you'll need to focus for the next two months on working up some new material and markets, or adding a part-time job to your schedule, or even considering—if things don't turn around—going back to a full-time day job.

Whatever you decide to do, consider the real causes that got you into this situation. You will likely learn enough to avoid its happening again.

Returning to the Working World

Should you find it necessary to return to the ranks of the conventional working world, be prepared for a shock. If you've written full-time more than a couple of months, the transition back can be difficult—rougher on you than making the transition to full-time writing.

Prepare for this by considering how your life has changed during the freelancing period. After you go back to a regular job, you won't be able to sleep in. And you can't take off on errands, or just relax whenever you wish.

And you may feel restricted—by a narrow job description, an insensitive boss, a work cubicle without your favorite music, even a dress code.

There are other negatives; I'm sure you can think of plenty. But at least one aspect may be a positive: being around other people all day. And you may find working a regular job a bit simpler than writing—you don't have to decide what to do, since your work is probably defined by others to a great degree.

And you'll probably appreciate tremendously the regular paycheck, and probably benefits, too. If you've been through some tough times financially as a full-time writer, you'll be relieved to be back in the salaried workforce, cashing that paycheck every week or two.

Once you're back into the regular ranks of working folks, remember: There are many ways to continue to fulfill the passion for writing that you undoubtedly still feel.

Journey's End?

The return to a full-time job doesn't mean the end of your journey as a writer. When your life is once again balanced, you should get back to your writing, just part-time now.

Surprisingly, you may find (again) that writing is more fun and more interesting if you don't have to depend on it for your living. You'll be free to explore side roads at will, and can venture into new territory—things you couldn't always afford to do when you were writing full-time. If you try something new and it doesn't work, you've lost nothing.

Second Time Around

If you leave behind your dream, will you ever have a second chance to become a full-time freelance writer? Yes. And if you do, you will certainly be better informed than when you first tried it. You will have much more experience the second time around, and should be better able to avoid the most common roadblocks and detours.

Getting back into it is a matter of once again preparing yourself to write full-time. This means getting your finances in order, building up new lists of writing credits, and meeting all the other criteria set forth throughout this book. However, you should not try writing full-time again, if:

- You haven't determined what went wrong the first time.

- You have young children or are responsible for someone who doesn't have a steady income.

- You have serious health problems or a long-term condition, and depend on your employer's health insurance.

If any of the above is true for you, writing full-time just may be too big a risk. The safer bet might be to focus on writing part-time.

"Still Crazy After All These Years . . ."

By now, you have figured out that I am no millionaire. And you've noticed my aversion to insecurity—especially the constant ups and downs.

So why would anyone voluntarily stick with this kind of life? The uncertainty alone is enough to stop many people from considering it. For example, I don't know that I'll ever be able to retire. (I tell myself that writing is too much fun to give up, anyway.) And at times I have found it nearly impossible to pay a house payment, insurance, or other recurring bill. Often, the crisis was only averted at the eleventh hour by the arrival of a long-awaited check for work completed long ago.

To avoid this, I often pay recurring bills ahead. But this means denying myself the pleasure of using the money as it's earned. Still, it's wonderful to have some bills paid six months in advance.

I never know how much I'll earn in a year. But I do believe it will usually be more than I could be making at a salaried job.

So overall, for me, the benefits outweigh the detriments. But I have to admit that the peaks and valleys can be unsettling to anyone expecting a calm, regular, predictable life.

The Peak of Contentment

My best year was definitely eventful. During one year of record income, I was more productive than I had ever been. I turned out four and one-half books, along with three dozen magazine pieces (plus some catalog copy-writing side jobs and a few other odd pieces of work).

At the same time, I spent more time away from home than during other years. Attending two trade shows and five conventions, plus a family trip to Disney World, should have limited my writing time. But it didn't.

I was bringing in so much money that I misplaced a $1,500 check and didn't miss it until much later, when I came across it while looking for something else.

I received a couple of nice honors that year—for my writing, and for some public-service activities with schools and scouts.

All in all, things were great. I paid up my house payments several months in advance, and had money left over—even after all the traveling. I had signed a contract for yet another book, and was rolling full-speed toward snaring a third lucrative magazine column. My short stories were selling, too—always a nice bonus, since I enjoy writing these so much.

The Valley of Despair

Two years later, I ran headlong into my worst year. Or, perhaps, it ran into me. After time and personal energy consumed by a divorce and auto accident, I got virtually no writing done. I had two book contracts, but could not get rolling on them, and thus delayed the advances due on delivery of the manuscripts.

That year I made only $17,000—most of that in the way of royalties on declining books that went out of print soon after. Due to financial difficulties, I came close to losing my new home.

From what I've learned in trading stories with other full-time

On Rewards

Work and thou canst not escape the reward; whether the work be fine or coarse, planting corn or writing epics, so only it be honest work, done to thine own approbation, it shall earn a reward to the senses as well as to the thought.
—Ralph Waldo Emerson

writers, the range of ups and downs I experienced during that span of three or so years is not uncommon.

The moral: Learn to plan around the averages. Don't get too excited (or lax) when the good things happen. And don't despair when the bad ones hit. Save enough money or work for a big downturn. And hang in there until things get better. Put everything into selling more and getting paid more.

That, or go out and find a job with a regular paycheck.

Why I'm Still at It

The writing life is far from perfect. Why do I stick with it? I list the reasons below—in no particular order, but in complete honesty:

- I like to stay up late and sleep in.

- Most years, I make more money freelancing than I could ever make at a regular job.

- The possibility of increasing that income to higher levels is always present.

- A close friend once characterized me as a "risk-taker." She was right. Putting myself—my creativity, my security, my finances—on the line just seems like the right road to take—for me.

- I love the ego boost I get when I'm signing autographs, reading fan mail, speaking at a writers' conference, and in general being in the public eye as a Writer. I'm gregarious, and I love to get out and meet more people than I would in a conventional occupation.

- There's no heavy lifting required.

- I'm never bored. My work is endlessly interesting, and often thoroughly fascinating.

- My time is my own. As you may have noticed, I've mentioned more than once the joy of being able to sleep in, even if it means occasional late hours at the computer keyboard.

- The fringe benefits include free books (since I do reviews), paid travel on occasion, and the chance to meet famous writers I've admired since my teens.

- There have been times when I believed I have succeeded in touching other peoples' lives through my writing, and readers have been so kind as to write to thank me.

In many ways, writing full-time allows me greater control of my life than would otherwise be possible. That measure of personal fulfillment is of immense value to me.

AFTERWORD

Well, here it is—your roadmap to a career as a full-time writer. You have learned about the detours and speed bumps ahead, realized there are some shortcuts, and discovered how to plan to make your journey in a reasonably safe way. The route you take now is up to you.

Traditionally, how-to books on writing are more formal than this one, and not nearly as autobiographical. I hope that my personalizing the journey made it more accessible to you. A full-time writing career involves a serious life-change, and it is best that you see the difficult as well as the easy and fun parts.

I might have avoided writing in detail about some of the pitfalls, but that would have done you a disservice. Just giving you platitudes and easy advice reveals nothing you don't already know.

Instead, I've tried to show you how your life may be affected by missteps and errors in judgment, and how it will be enriched by making the right moves. A lot has happened to me, some of it good and some of it bad. I've tried to appreciate the good while learning from the bad. And now I have shared my experience with you. I hope you've gained a realistic attitude about your potential for success—and have some better ideas now about how to achieve that.

To succeed as a writer, you need to be confident in your abilities. You have to be hungry to write—and to embrace the crazy, exhilarating life of a freelancer. You must be aware of the risks—and just fearful enough to want to work hard to avoid them.

If I've inspired you to succeed as a full-time writer, or helped make the route a bit smoother, I've achieved my goal. And if you've decided to remain a part-time freelancer, and this book manages to help you do that better—and feel better about it—I'll be happy with that, too.

Full-time freelance writing isn't for everyone. But for those of us who have chosen it as a way to make a living, we love it wholeheartedly, and are willing to share it with any of you ready to embark on this great adventure.

Ultimately, the destination is the journey itself.

That's it—it's time to hit the road!

Resources for Writers

The range of writers' organizations covers just about every sort of writing there is. If I omitted one that you feel to be important, feel free to contract me with any suggestion addition to future editions of this book. Send e-mail to the publisher at writerbooks@kalmbach.com, or to me at WritingCareer@aol.com.

Writers' Organizations

Academy of American Poets
Web site: http://www.poets.org/

American Crime Writers League (ACWL)
455 Crescent
Buffalo, NY 14214
E-mail: dougand@aol.com
Web site: http://www.acwl.org/
(Includes fiction and nonfiction.)

American Society of Journalists and Authors (ASJA)
1501 Broadway, Suite 302
New York, NY 10036
Phone: (212) 997-0947
E-mail: asja@compuserve.com
Web site: http://www.asja.org/

Black Writers Alliance (BWA)
P.O. Box 700065
Dallas, TX 75370-0065
E-mail: TiaShabazz@Blackwriters.org
Web site: http://www.blackwriters.org/

Canadian Association of Journalists (CAJ)
St. Patrick's Building, Carleton University
1125 Colonel By Drive
Ottawa, Ontario K1S 5B6
Canada
Phone: (613) 526-8061
E-mail: caj@igs.net
Web site: http://eagle.ca/caj/

Canadian Authors Association (CAA)
Box 419
Campbellford, Ontario K0L 1L0
Canada
E-mail: canauth@redden.on.ca
Web site: http://www.canauthors.org/national.html

The Canadian Romance Authors Network (CRAN)
E-mail: lsimmons23@home.com
Web site: http://www.canadianromanceauthors.com/

Crime Writers of Canada (CWC)
E-mail: info@crimewriterscanada.com
Web site: http://www.crimewriterscanada.com/

Editorial Freelancers Association
71 W. 23rd St., Suite 1910
New York, NY 10010-4102
Phone: (212) 929-5400 / (866) 929-5400
E-mail: info@the-efa.org
Web site: http://www.the-efa.org

Horror Writers Association (HWA)
P.O. Box 50577
Palo Alto, CA 94303
E-mail: hwa@horror.org
Web site: http://www.horror.org/

International Women's Writing Guild (IWWG)
P.O. Box 810, Gracie Station
New York, NY 10028-0082
Phone: (212) 737-7536
E-mail: dirhahn@aol.com
Web site: http://www.iwwg.com/

Mystery Writers of America (MWA)
17 E. 47th St., 6th Floor
New York, NY 10017
Phone: (212) 888-8171
E-mail: mwa_org@earthlink.net
Web site: http://www.mysterywriters.org/

National Association of Science Writers (NASW)
P.O. Box 890
Hedgesville, WV 25427
Phone: (304) 754-5077
E-mail: diane@nasw.org
Web site: http://nasw.org/

National Writers Association (NWA)
3140 S. Peoria St., #295 PMB
Aurora, CO 80014
Phone: (303) 841-0246
Web site: http://www.nationalwriters.com/

The National Writers Union AFL/CIO
113 University Pl., 6th Floor
New York, NY 10003
E-mail: nwu@nwu.org
Phone: (212) 254-0279
Web site: http://www.nwu.org/

Novelists, Inc.
P.O. Box 1166
Mission, KS 66222-0166
Email: ninc@kc.rr.com
Web site: http://www.ninc.com

Outdoor Writers Association of America
121 Hickory St., Suite 1
Missoula, MT 59801
Phone: (406) 728-7434
E-mail: intern@montana.com
Web site: http://www.owaa.org/

PEN American Center
568 Broadway
New York, NY 10012
Phone: (212) 334-1660
E-mail: pen@pen.org
Web site: http://www.pen.org/

Romance Writers of America (RWA)
3707 FM 1960 W., Suite 555
Houston, TX 77068
Phone: (281) 440-6885
E-mail: info@rwanational.com
Web site: http://www.rwanational.com

Science Fiction and Fantasy Writers of America (SFWA)
P.O. Box 877
Chestertown, MD 21620
E-mail: execdir@sfwa.org
Web site: http://www.sfwa.org/

Society of Children's Book Writers and Illustrators
(SCBWI)
8271 Beverly Blvd.
Los Angeles, CA 90048
Phone: (323) 782-1010
E-mail: membership@scbwi.org
Web site: http://www.scbwi.org/

Society of Professional Journalists (SPJ)
3909 N. Meridian St.
Indianapolis, IN 46208
Phone: (317) 927-8000, ext. 216
E-Mail: jgrimes@spj.org
Web site:http://www.spj.org/

Western Writers of America (WWA)
209 E. Iowa
Cheyenne, WY 82009
E-mail: hogranch@msn.com
Web site: http://www.westernwriters.org/

Writers Guild of America (WGA East)
555 W. 57th St.
New York, NY 10019
Phone: (212) 767-7800
Web site: http://www.wgaeast.org

Writers Guild of America (WGA West)
8955 Beverly Blvd.
West Hollywood, CA 90048
Phone: (310) 550-1000
Web site: http://www.wga.org/

Writers Guild of Canada (WGC)
123 Edward St., Suite 1225
Toronto, Ontario M5G 1E2
Canada
Phone: (416) 979-7907 or (800) 567-9974
Email: info@wgc.ca
Web site: http://www.writersguildofcanada.com/

Online Resources for Writers

It is impossible to list all Web sites of interest to writers. They're too numerous, and a good percentage will change URLs by the time you read this book. Some will disappear.

One of the best ways to keep up with changes and new sites of interest is to use search engines. AltaVista (http://www.altavista.digital.com/), Google (http://www.google.com), and Hotbot (http://www.hotbot.com) are easy to use and provide excellent lists. Search using the keyword "writers" or the phrase "writers' group," and you'll find more sites than you can visit in a week.

In addition, *The Writer* magazine has an excellent Web site, at http://www.writermag.com, with useful links in addition to its wealth of information, advice, and guidance for freelancers.

Here's a list of sites that are likely to offer good information, contacts, and links to other Web sites for writers for some time to come.

Absolute Write
http://www.absolutewrite.com

AJR Newslink
http://ajr.newslink.org/

AuthorLink
http://www.authorlink.com/

Association of Authors' Representatives (AAR)
http:www.aar-online.org

BookWeb.org (American Booksellers Association)
http://www.bookweb.org/

Children's Writing Resource Center
http://www.write4kids.com/

Editor & Publisher Online
http://www.mediainfo.com/

Guide to Literary Agents
www.literaryagents.org

Literary Market Place
www.literarymarketplace.com

The Market List
http://www.marketlist.com/
The Mining Co. freelance writers' site
http://freelancewrite.miningco.com

Newslink
http://newslink.org/

Poets & Writers Online
http://www.pw.org/

Publishers Weekly
http://www.publishersweekly.com/

The Write News
http://www.writenews.com/

The Writer Online
http://www.writermag.com

Writers Write
http://www.writerswrite.com/

WritersNet: Writers, Editors, Agents, Publishers
www.writers.net

Writing-World.com
http://www.writing-world.com

Web Resources for the Self-Employed

1st Insurance Quotes
http://1stinsurancequotes.com/

Canada Customs and Revenue Agency (CCRA)
http://www.ccra-adrc.gc.ca
Health Insurance Resource Center
http://www.healthinsurance.org

Internal Revenue Service (IRS)
http://www.irs.gov/

National Association of the Self-Employed (NASE)
http://www.nase.org

National Business Association (NBA)
http://www.nationalbusiness.org/

Self-Employed Country (CA for the Self-Employed)
http://www.selfemployedcountry.org/

Suggested Reading

As with any profession, writers need to stay up-to-date not only on markets, but also on the mechanics of writing well, how to market your work, the business of writing, and more. Every writer can find ways to improve what he or she does, and reading any of the following books is a good way to broaden one's knowledge.

Agents and Marketing

The American Directory of Writer's Guidelines: What Editors Want, What Editors Buy, edited by John C. Mutchler (Quill River Books, 1997)

Be Your Own Literary Agent: The Ultimate Insider's Guide to Getting Published, third edition, by Martin P. Levin (Ten Speed Press, 2002)

The Career Novelist: A Literary Agent Offers Strategies for Success, by Donald Maass (Heineman, 1996)

How to Be Your Own Literary Agent: The Business of Getting a Book Published, revised edition, by Richard Curtis (Mariner Books, 1996)

Literary Agents: The Essential Guide for Writers, by Debby Mayer (Penguin Books)

Marketing Strategies for Writers, by Michael Sedge (Allworth Press, 1999)

The Writer's Guide to Queries, Pitches & Proposals, by Moira Allen (Allworth Press, 2001)

Writing.com: Creative Internet Strategies to Advance Your Writing Career, by Moira Allen (Allworth Press, 1999)

Market Directories

Children's Writer's & Illustrator's Market (Writer's Digest Books, annual)

The Christian Writers' Market Guide (Harold Shaw Publishers)

Guide to Literary Agents (Writer's Digest Books, annual)

The Internet Writer's Handbook 2001/2, by Karen Scott (Allison & Busby, 2001)

Literary Market Place (Information Today, Inc., annual)

Novel and Short Story Writer's Market (Writer's Digest Books)

Poet's Market (Writer's Digest Books, annual)

The Writer's Guide to Book Editors, Publishers, and Literary Agents, by Jeff Herman (The Writer Books, annual)

The Writer's Handbook (The Writer Books, annual)

Writer's Market: Where & How to Sell What You Write (Writer's Digest Books, annual)

Writer's Online Marketplace (Writer's Digest Books, annual)

Autobiographies and Memoirs

Another Life, by Michael Korda (Random House, 1999)

Education of a Wandering Man, by Louis L'Amour (Bantam Books, 1990 reissue)

On Writing: A Memoir of the Craft, by Stephen King (Scribner, 2002)

The Way the Future Was, by Frederik Pohl (Del Rey Books, 1978)

Business Guides for Writers

The Book Publishing Industry, by Albert N. Greco (Allyn & Bacon, 1996)

Every Writer's Guide to Copyright and Publishing Law, by Ellen M. Kozak (Owlet, 1997)

The Magazine Publishing Industry, by Charles P. Daly, Patrick Henry, and Ellen Ryder (Allyn & Bacon, 1996)

Mastering the Business of Writing, by Richard Curtis (Allworth Press, 1996)

This Business of Publishing: An Insider's View of Current Trends and Tactics, by Richard Curtis (Allworth Press, 1998)

The Writer's Legal Guide, by Tad Crawford and Tony Lyons (Allworth Press, 1998)

Reference Books

Advice to Writers: A Compendium of Quotes, Anecdotes, and Writerly Wisdom from a Dazzling Array of Literary Lights, ed. by Jon Winokur (Vintage, 2000)

A Dictionary of English and Romance Languages Equivalent Proverbs, by Teodor Flonta (DeProverbio.com, 2001)

English Through the Ages, by William Brohaugh (Writer's Digest Books, 1998)

Roget's Thesaurus, indexed sixth edition, by Barbara Ann Kipfer (HarperCollins, 2001)

Roget's Thesaurus of Phrases, by Barbara Ann Kipfer (Writer's Digest Books, 2002)

Synonym Finder, revised edition, by J. I. Rodale, Nancy Laroche, and Faye C. Allen (Warner Books, 1986)

The Write Book: An Illustrated Treasury of Tips, Tactics and Tirades, ed. by Bob Perlongo (Art Direction Book Co., 2002)

Writer's Digest Flip Dictionary, by Barbara Ann Kipfer (Writer's Digest Books)

Writer's Encyclopedia, third edition, by the editors of Writer's Digest (Writer's Digest Books, 2003)

The Writer's Guide to Research: An Invaluable Guide to Gathering Material for Articles, Novels and Non-Fiction Books, second edition, by Marion Field (Trans-Atlantic Publications, Inc, 2000)

The Writer's Quotation Book, fourth edition, James Charlton, Editor (Faber & Faber, 1997)

Books for the Beginning Freelance Writer

The Elements of Authorship: Unabashed Advice, Undiluted Experience, and Unadulterated Inspiration for Writers and Writers-to-be, by Arthur Plotnik (toExcel Press/iUniverse, 2000)

Starting Your Career as a Freelance Writer, by Moira Allen (Allworth Press, 2003)

Write on Target: A Five-Phase Program for Nonfiction Writers, by Dennis E. Hensley and Holly G. Miller (The Writer, Inc. 1995)

Advanced Techniques

The Elements of Editing: A Modern Guide for Editors and Journalists, by Arthur Plotnik (Collier Books/Macmillan Publishing Co., 1982).

How to Write Fast (While Writing Well), by David Fryxell (Writer's Digest Books)

Ready, Aim, Specialize!: Create Your Own Writing Specialty and Make More Money, by Kelly James-Enger (The Writer Books, 2003)

Writing & Revising Your Fiction, by Mark Wisniewski (The Writer Books)

Magazines

This list includes some key magazines of particular value to freelance writers. They are available by subscription, at your local bookstore or newsstand, or at your local library.

Editor & Publisher
http://www.editorandpublisher.com/

Poets & Writers
http://www.pw.org/

Publishers Weekly
http://www.publishersweekly.com

The Writer
http://www.writermag.com

Writer's Digest
http://www.writersdigest

The Writer

The Writer was founded in 1887 by two reporters from the *Boston Globe*. Their mission was to publish a magazine that would be "helpful, interesting, and instructive to all literary workers." The magazine soon became an essential resource for writers, publishing articles in the first half of the 20th century by literary luminaries such as William Carlos Williams, Wallace Stegner, Sinclair Lewis, William Saroyan, Daphne du Maurier, and many others.

After a long editorial tenure into the latter half of the 20th century by A. S. Burack and then Sylvia K. Burack, Kalmbach Publishing Co. purchased the magazine in the year 2000, along with its affiliated line of books on writing fiction and nonfiction, and moved the editorial operations from Boston to Waukesha, Wisconsin, a suburb of Milwaukee.

Continuing its long heritage of more than 110 years of service now into the 21st century, *The Writer* magazine continues to be an essential resource for writers, providing advice from our most prominent writers, featuring informative articles about the art and the business of writing.

It is dedicated to helping and inspiring writers to succeed in their endeavors and to fostering a sense of community among writers everywhere.

More information on *The Writer,* with current articles and other resources, can be found online at the Web site http://www.writermag.com.

—Elfrieda Abbe, Editor
The Writer